The Agathon Engine

A World-Building
Primer for the 2020s

Fourth Wave Initiative

HORNGATE

First edition published by
Horngate Media
New Port Richey, FL 34653
USA

ISBN: 978-0-9909700-7-1

Book Layout & Pre-Press:
Philip H. Farber
http://www.hawkridgeproductions.com

Cover Design:
Gregory K. Koon

"You never change things by fighting the existing reality. To change something, build a new model that makes the existing model obsolete." - Buckminster Fuller

Contents

SECTION ONE: OBJECTIVES AND VALUES

The Fourth Wave and the Agathon Engine 1
Ipseity 9
Expression 11
Becoming 15
Sovereignty 21
Spontanous Order 27
Institutions 35
Property 49
Technology 55
Enclaves 63
Creating the Context 71

SECTION TWO: STRATEGIC FRAMES

The Shift 77
The Source 81
The Network 87
The Hack 91
The Upgrade 99
The Bloom 103
The Cosmos 109

SECTION THREE: SCALABLE TOOLS

The Mastermind Platform 119
Remedial Memeology 123
Nonprofit Organizations 131
Engaging Media 137
Forming Coalitions and Joint Ventures 145

SECTION ONE:

OBJECTIVES AND VALUES

1

The Fourth Wave and
the Agathon Engine

In this initial essay, we present a concept for the future and a few seed-ideas concerning it, addressed primarily to people who already know something of what is happening in the world today, and so can most easily grasp the simple points made here and who will be in the best positions to act upon them. It is not especially visionary - what it describes is generally already happening. The issue is that it is mostly happening unconsciously, and so this communication is simply an initial call to the right people who can act with the right awareness to gently steer the forces at play into their best realization.

When Alvin Toffler wrote his book *The Third Wave*, he described human history as being defined by three technological waves that each radically transformed human society, culture and civilization. These were settled agriculture, industrialization and computerization (this last being relatively new at the time the book was written). From spans of millennia to centuries, the intervals between waves have accelerated, so it is not unreasonable to see the emergence of a Fourth Wave only a few decades after Toffler heralded the emergence of the Third Wave.

To understand what the Fourth Wave is, consider fire and everything that has followed from the human mastery and application of it through diverse technologies to the variety of human needs and desires. Next, think about how consciousness, reason and creativity are often metaphorically viewed as a kind of light or fire. The Fourth Wave is the mastery and application of this 'Mind-Fire' as a real, tangible and practical technology in the same way that literal fire and electricity have been mastered and applied.

When we say "technology" here, it is important to define it as inclusively as possible. Models and techniques as well as machines. Both software and hardware in the broadest sense of the terms. All of this technology together constitutes what Kevin Kelly calls the "Technium". The Mind-Fire and the Technium influence and shape each other reciprocally through their ongoing interaction.

It must then be pointed out that the Fourth Wave is something essentially different from the previous three. Fourth Wave technologies have existed from the beginning and right along through history - language, art, books and so on - and it was, of course, the

Mind-Fire that drove the developments in agriculture, industry and computation. Rather than being discrete phenomena, we can see the First, Second and Third Waves as the major phases of a more general technological wave that is the material wake of a spirally accelerating Mind-Fire meta-wave. The term "Fourth Wave" may then also be understood as referring to the emergence of this meta-wave in its pure and explicit form.

It ultimately refers to the possibility of the Mind-Fire's absolute liberation and mastery.

Former hunter-gatherers developing agriculture had no way to know what life in city-states would be like, and agrarian people had no way to extrapolate a culture of automobiles, airplanes and televisions from the cotton gin. We have the advantage with the first three waves of viewing them in hindsight, so things are much more clear. When it comes to the Fourth Wave, though, we are in the same position as our ancestors and really have no way to know what existence will be like mere decades from now. The best that we can do is to take some core values and act in accord with them as our best means of surfing this wave of incredibly radical change rather than being swept away by it.

The Greek word *agathon* means "good" or "beautiful" and is used in philosophy as a term for the highest or supreme Good.

This is humanity's highest ideal - the Ideal of ideals - and the history of the world has been touched by an innumerable variety of initiatives or movements aimed at being, doing or creating Good. However, while we can discern historical trends of general improvement in all areas of human existence, much of the progress seems haphazard, sometimes only temporary, and we can also see several occasions where dreams of utopia have turned into nightmares of oppression. As a result, the explicit pursuit of the Good is now often seen as naive at best or as dangerous and sinister at worst.

Much study and long periods of meditation on the subject have revealed what appears to be the common, fatal flaw in failed attempts to create the Good. In these cases, a vision of the Good (which may or may not be sound) originates with one person or a small group who either possesses or obtains the power to impose the vision in a uniform, top-down way upon others. All such cases are examples of what Virginia Postrel has called "One Best Way" thinking and seem to actually contradict the Good.

For the purposes of this project, pursuing a real understanding of the Good and how to promote it requires a new line of thought.

We learn from economics that value is subjective and relative to a specific valuer. A thing is only 'good' in that it enhances the existence of a particular entity from the perspective of that particular entity. In proposing such a profound Object as THE Good, it must be balanced by an equally profound Subject: this singular and essential Good is the Good of a singular and essential entity. However, the implicit differences among sapient beings cause a seeming paradox that must be transcended. If we are to propose a singular, essential and yet *decentralized* Good, that Good must be the enhancement of Individual existence.

From this position, we can make a number of statements about some basic values that support the Good and how they may expand it.

1. The process of expanding the Good must begin with the primary element or unit involved: the essential and monadic IPSEITY or Selfhood of the Individual being.

2. The unique existence of the Individual calls for the discovery and EXPRESSION of personal power and a

sense of Life Purpose that most fully enhance and fulfill the unique potential of that personal existence.

3. In actualizing and fulfilling its potential and sense of purpose, each Individual has a unique process of growth, development or BECOMING to pursue.

4. The SOVEREIGNTY of the Individual in personal and social affairs, expressed as Self-Ownership, Self-Reliance and Self-Determinism, follows from the needs for Expression and Becoming that derive from Ipseity.

5. SPONTANEOUS ORDER, resulting from voluntary and non-aggressive association and exchange among Individuals, is the proper form of society in reflecting the Sovereignty of its participants.

6. The maintenance of this society calls for the preservation, optimization and further establishment of dynamic INSTITUTIONS that reflect and support all of the principles or elements described in these statements.

7. PROPERTY is the reflection and extension of the Ipseity and Expression of the Individual within material substance, and the means for preserving Individual Sovereignty within a voluntary system of

social order.

8. As a material extension of personal power and intention, TECHNOLOGY is crucially important as means for facilitating the Expression and Becoming of the Individual, exchanges of value among Individuals, the transformation of environments and the general enhancement of existence.

9. The practical combination of Individual Sovereignty and Spontaneous Order with Property and Technology results in the formation of diverse, autonomous ENCLAVES and environments that support the fulfilment of the Good of the inhabitants and provide platforms for its further growth and evolution.

These things are stated here briefly and directly to proclaim our positions and define our areas of interest and endeavor. They should not, however, be thought to emerge as decrees from the aether without explanation or commentary. There are past history and lineages of thought behind each of these statements, as well as much room for exploration in how they may be applied to the present and future.

This is the work that lies before us and we hope to be *Good* at it.

What is being called the Fourth Wave here is a way of looking at and understanding trends and needs that already exist and will continue to become much more important in the very near future. However, the very idea or meme of "The Fourth Wave" is also a Fourth Wave tool in itself, a focusing lens that makes those trends and needs more consciously explicit for the sake of organizing thought, effort and resources around them so as to facilitate their best emergence and fulfillment.

That is to say, that the more that Individuals working in these areas think in terms of the Fourth Wave and pursue that work specifically in terms of the Fourth Wave, the more quickly the Fourth Wave will manifest, the more powerfully and harmoniously it will manifest, the more ready we will all be for it and the more we will all benefit from it.

2

Ipseity

"The process of expanding the Good must begin with the primary element or unit involved: the essential and monadic IPSEITY or Selfhood of the Individual being."

The word "ipseity" refers to the sense of personal identity, individuality or Selfhood. It comes from the Latin *ipse,* meaning "Self". We might as easily use the word Selfhood but for an important distinction that should be made. For our purposes here, we are not talking about personal identity in the sense of our thoughts and feelings, likes and dislikes, roles or circumstances. We will get to those later, but it is important to begin with the immanent, core Self that is only a monad or point of perception and intention. The distinction is aided by using a precise word that does not have the colloquial associations attached to all the other terms.

This is the ultimate basis of the *Individual* in the literal sense of being *undividable.* Whether we personally believe it to be a pre-existent spiritual essence or an emergent property of the neuroelectric maelstrom (or both, or neither), our essential experience of ourselves is as an Entity that experiences. As explained earlier, this is the root of all value as a concept before even getting into what specific things are valued. Value only exists relative to a valuer. Without an Experiencer, nothing at all matters at all. That is why we must start here, at the actual start, before moving into secondary or tertiary forms of identity. It is the primary element or unit involved in any consideration of any mode of life or social system - the actual Experiencer of that mode or system!

First and foremost, we Self-value the Experiencer.

This is the ultimate in 'first principles' thinking and we can consciously then unfold every value that follows from this essential starting point, which is exactly what we are going to do. While this understanding of the Self is rather abstract, it will be further explicated and materialized progressively through each of the following values as their fundamental, underlying basis.

This makes for a very short chapter, but it is of the most essential importance. There are only so many words that one can say about a monadic point of pure, subjective awareness with no other qualities in itself, but it is the peg upon which everything else hangs.

3

Expression

"The unique existence of the Individual calls for the discovery and EXPRESSION of personal power and a sense of Life Purpose that most fully enhance and fulfill the unique potential of that personal existence."

The Self is, in itself, ultimately detached and removed from phenomena but possesses the complementary root-faculties of perception and intention as media of interaction and experience. Through the receptive faculty of perception, Self experiences itself as a Self through distinction from not-Self - Subject and object(s) - in that anything that can be perceived is Other. On the more active side of intention, the Self experiences itself even more distinctly as a Self when it acts with agency and volition against the drift of its surrounding milieu.

Every Self, then, is at core a unique and transcendent viewpoint for the perception of phenomena and correspondingly forms unique sets of intentions from those perceptions relative to that unique viewpoint. Together, these perceptions and intentions form the basis of a unique expression of Essence-in-Action.

The philosopher Friedrich Nietzsche put it very well when he said that a living being seeks above all to discharge its strength. This is what we mean here by Expression. It is the engagement of our abstract sense of Ipseity with the kaleidoscopic, textural stuff of experience, our development of meaning from that engagement (and vice-versa) and our pursuit of pleasure within that context, all as a creative expression of that "I AM" distinction.

Where the term Ipseity refers to our *Essence* - the primal distinction of Self - its extension through Expression is our *Being*: our perceptions, our intentions, our thoughts, our feelings, our aesthetics, our desires, our actions and our general style of life. Effected consciously, this includes learning and is the unfolding of sapience from sentience, which plays out in our Becoming and every other principle or value that follows in this text.

Without Expression, the Self (in its Ipseity), remains locked up in a tower, so to speak; and to the extent that its unique Expression is restricted, it experiences frustration and alienation. This is the experience of restricted or diminished Being. On the other hand, the free outflow of Expression increases the experience of Being. This discharge of strength in Expression shows the ultimately creative role of the Self. With every Self being a Creator that works and expands from a different initial viewpoint, the existence of multiple Creators naturally tends toward great differentiation in Beings.

It can be seen, then, that Expression bridges our isolate Self to all of our experience and also sets up the basic social situation that will become so important as we proceed: the harmonization of experience among greatly differentiated Beings.

4

Becoming

"In actualizing and fulfilling its potential and sense of purpose, each Individual has a unique process of growth, development or BECOMING to pursue."

Since at least the Renaissance, 'human nature' has often been defined somewhat paradoxically by its adaptability and mutability. In his *Oratio de hominis dignitate* (Oration on the Dignity of Man), Giovanni Pico della Mirandola observed that Man is more or less a blank slate with no particular nature of his own or place in the natural order by comparison with the (other) animals, whose natures and existences are predetermined. Pico may have lacked our present genetic and evolutionary knowledge on how some personal traits and social tendencies are to an extent inborn, but his main point that Man has the freedom and capability to create his own nature and role in the world as he will through his own efforts still applies for both the singular human and the species as a whole.

Earlier, we referenced Nietzsche's idea that discharging its strength is the primary aim of a living being. This discharge of strength manifests as an inner dynamic that defines the flow of desire or purpose within us that in turn defines our life path toward the highest expression and fulfilment of what becomes our own nature. You have probably heard some variation of the saying that thoughts and desires become beliefs and values, which become actions, which become character, which becomes destiny.

Picture in your mind a tree or a coral. In the shapes and colors of their branches - their outward, reaching growth - you can plainly and simply see motion and manifestation simultaneously. You can understand how Expression, as it builds up momentum and substance, becomes Becoming.

With that image in mind, you can also understand how personal Expression flowing from a unique sense of Ipseity forms a unique trajectory of Becoming. With everyone having this unique trajectory of their own, there is differentiation of people. The more people there are, the more differentiation there is. Or at least there should be. Human societies can have a perverse tendency toward homogenization, which is a mistake.

Look at the one area where differentiation is most (but not absolutely) encouraged: the division of labor. When we talk about hunter-gatherer societies, there is a reason that we call them that - very few career opportunities. More differentiation came with agriculture, and more with industrialization. Now, people have careers that not only did not exist a generation ago but could not have existed. This is cumulative creation and expansion just within what many people (perhaps mistakenly) disdain as the most quotidian and 'bottom line' area of existence, but it derives from increasing differentiation of Expression and Becoming while then providing the platform for more.

Natural, biological evolution is completely crazy for differentiation and we should be, too, for the same reasons. It provides resilience and antifragility. Moreover, though, in a society and culture that embraces Ipseity, Expression and Becoming as essential values and thus defines us as Creators, it is the actual *point* of the culture - and this is what we are working to support and further.

Once again, we want to make a distinction, this time between the person that we might become through the unconscious and haphazard drift of existence and who we might Become by consciously and intentionally taking hold of the wheel. Our varied Expressions of our inner dynamic, informed and guided by our Ipseity as what John Lilly called the

"Self-metaprogrammer of the human biocomputer", empowers and organizes our manifested Becoming.

It is not just a personal process but also a collaborative one through social interactions and exchanges, and through culture. This is why humanity has no specific place in the animal order, as Pico observed. Our place is adaptive, mutable, and essentially imaginative, as we are fundamentally the hands in the clay of ongoing Creation. Our *telos* is a moving target: the continuing creation and recreation of ourselves and of external worlds and worlds-within-worlds.

A few words should be said about the subject of psychology. Before *The Third Wave*, Alvin Toffler wrote a book called *Future Shock* about the psychological effects upon both Individuals and society of what is perceived as too much change in too short a time. The thing about that is, the potential for future shock that might have affected Toffler's readers 50 years ago was negligible in comparison to what the world will experience in the next decade. The increase is, itself, increasing.

Look at where we already are now. People in the developed world live in the closest thing to utopia in all of human history, but increasingly claim to suffer from stress and anxiety. The whole world is connected through instantaneous communication, but there is an increasing 'loneliness epidemic'. People seem to be lacking more and more in the key psychological areas of meaning, engagement and pleasure. If our current psychological understanding is not addressing these issues or their causes now, they will certainly be more ineffective - if not totally useless - in the face of what is coming. A radical, Fourth Wave update and upgrade of therapeutic psychology is a survival imperative.

On the other hand, though, we also know that when psychology does address therapeutic needs, it next moves into personal optimization and Self-actualization. We see this in the work of men like Abraham Maslow and Carl Jung, where psychology goes beyond healing and into what we might call - to borrow an archaic term - Initiation. This form of Becoming is crucial to existence in the world that is emerging.

Ipseity, Expression and Becoming tell us the absolute essentials of who we are and what we are doing, and so are the root-values of our entire project. All of the social and cultural values that will be described next are derived from these root-values. They are shaped by them, informed by them, honor them and sustain them in the organization and manifestation of our collaborative efforts in that creative process.

5

Sovereignty

"The SOVEREIGNTY of the Individual in personal and social affairs, expressed as Self-Ownership, Self-Reliance and Self-Determinism, follows from the needs for Expression and Becoming that derive from Ipseity."

The next step follows directly from the others but takes us into a new dimension, the social one.

Over the course of transformation from the fertilized egg in the womb to the wizened figure in the hospice bed, everyone becomes something. For our purposes here, however, we are interested in those forms of Becoming rooted in Self-reflective awareness of personal existence and those decisions made and actions taken to consciously design or expand that existence. And it is an absolutely personal process. As such, it demands increasing levels of Self-knowledge and the liberty to act accordingly. This is Sovereignty.

To be *sovereign* is to own yourself, to "reign over" your own existence. It means to regulate and direct the affairs of your own life and to live your life as you want to live it, by your own values.

Each and every Individual is (at least potentially) a new and unique force in the world. No one person has ever or will ever possess the same precise mix of perspective, knowledge, desire, intention and ability possessed by another. Until we have tried, even we do not fully know what we can be or do. From all this, as we have established, each Individual has their own unique nature and purposes in life.

Nietzsche's idea of the primary aim of a living organism being the discharge of its strength is a matter of power and liberty. He also said:

"My idea is that every specific body strives to be master over all space and to extend its force (its will to power) and to thrust back all that resists its extension. But it continually encounters similar efforts on the part of other bodies and ends by coming to an arrangement ('union') with those of them that are sufficiently related to it: Thus they conspire together for power."

Relatedly, in his book *The Tao of Power*, R.L. Wing states:

"Lao Tzu believed that when people do not have a sense of power they become resentful and uncooperative. Individuals who do not feel personal power feel fear...Lao Tzu attributed most of the world's ills to the fact that people do not feel

powerful and independent."

This reference to Laozi (Lao Tzu) is not a random appeal to authority, as the Daoist perspective becomes very important in the next chapter and is conjoined with the Nietzschean one in the next chapter after that.

Sovereignty is liberty and, more to the point, the active exercise of liberty in the expression of personal agency and power. It is the exercise of personal authority. Only you can legitimately speak for you. Your essential nature, needs and desires can only truly be known by you. The proper course and style of your life can only truly be determined by you. You are the sovereign authority with regard to your own mind and actions. And this is all true for everyone else, as well.

This understanding of Sovereignty is the basis for our concept of inalienable rights, which are rights that are not given as privileges or rewards by a crown or state but are inherent to a human being by virtue of human nature - whether that nature is interpreted as the work of Pico's God in his *Oratio*, "Nature's God" as conceived by Thomas Jefferson in the *Declaration of Independence*, biological evolution as understood by Ayn Rand in underlying her Objectivist Ethics (*The Virtue of Selfishness*), or whatever its source may have been. It simply is what it is, as people say.

Respect for the Sovereignty of Individuals is expressed in ethics by an axiom or principle that is best known as the Non-Aggression Principle. According to this principle, aggression is defined as the initiation of force against another Individual or their property. This initiation of force is seen to be a violation of the Sovereignty of others. Expressed the other way around, as a positive, this ethical principle is also known as Voluntarism.

Recognizing the Sovereignty of other Individuals provides the foundation for ethical social interactions. To respect the Sovereignty of others indicates a respect for Sovereignty as a general principle, which strengthens your understanding and appreciation of your own Sovereignty.

To disrespect the Sovereignty of others indicates a disrespect for Sovereignty, itself, which undermines the legitimacy of your own. Attempting to hold a dissonant viewpoint that asserts personal Sovereignty while performing or endorsing actions that violate the like status of other Individuals is a hypocrisy that will sunder the integrity of being.

We can see that mutual respect for the Sovereignty of

Individuals is the foundation of a free and right order in society if we understand it as the synthesis of the root-values of Ipseity, Expression and Becoming, and in turn as the root of the following organizing-values as the key to appropriate interpersonal relation and association.

Strangely, many people seem to have come to believe that society is an entity in itself, that it has a reality that is equal to - or, as some would have it, greater than - the reality of the Individuals that make it up. In this view, 'Society' is like a collective machine or body made up of subsidiary human parts or cells.

This 'organicism' is an example of what is known as a Reification Fallacy, where an abstraction or hypothetical construct is treated as if it were a concrete phenomenon or physical entity. In this particular case, it is also a blatantly inverted and backward view. The concept 'Society' is, in truth, merely a label for the sum of the interactions between Individuals. It is a dynamic, vibrant mass of living activity that is defined by its parts rather than defining them.

The greatest society would be one in which this is understood and acknowledged, with each Individual bringing forth the totality of the best within them and sharing and exchanging it in voluntary synergy with others, with society then being allowed to take its form more fluidly from those interactions.

Mutual respect among Sovereigns establishes the balance of freedom and stability that makes such a society possible.

6

Spontaneous Order

"SPONTANEOUS ORDER, resulting from voluntary and non-aggressive association and exchange among Individuals, is the proper form of society in reflecting the Sovereignty of its participants."

Spontaneous Order is the novel state or pattern that emerges from the free interaction of elements within a system. It is also sometimes described as Self-Organization or Emergence. As a process, Spontaneous Order allows for evolution through variation, competition, feedback and adaptation. It is dynamic and tends to overflow with abundance as many new and unexpected innovations emerge from its rich complexity. Examples of Spontaneous Order include ecosystems, neural networks, the evolution of language and free economic markets.

As our political and business cultures become increasingly mired in the centralization of power, top-down decision-making structures and obsessive micromanagement, it is not surprising if Spontaneous Order is still a somewhat obscure subject in our present society. However, it has been understood in several contexts by a variety of observers for a very long time.

Perhaps the earliest to write about it were the Daoist

philosophers of ancient China, notably Laozi and Zhuangzhi (also commonly known as Lao Tzu and Chuang Tzu). Laozi wrote that to grasp the world is to lose it and that the world is won by letting things alone. Zhuangzhi, in particular, emphasized that good order results spontaneously when things are let alone. Through these observations, the concept of *wu-wei* emerged as one of the most central Daoist teachings. This term, *wu-wei*, is often translated as "non-action".

This translation can be a bit confusing, so let us examine the term in more detail. It has two parts, where *wu* simply means a lack or absence, and *wei* refers to artificial, contrived action that interferes with the natural and spontaneous flow or development of the process at hand. A better translation for *wu-wei*, then, might be "non-interference" or "non-intervention".

Quite simply, for the Individual, it means keeping out of your own way. If you are, for example, an artist or musician, you will understand this concept immediately. Obviously, in these roles, you do ACT when you practice, create and perform. However, you are probably familiar with what can happen when you try to force the processes of creation and performance. You can trip yourself up and even shut the whole thing down completely. The fact is that this same thing applies for everyone, and in all facets of life.

It is also easy to see how Spontaneous Order works in the natural world. Each organism follows its own nature in the pursuit of survival, and its actions result in either success or failure. In the process, each organism adjusts its activities for greater success, and all of these activities settle into an optimal pattern that we call an *ecosystem* (where *eco-* derives from the Greek *oikos*, meaning "home", as also seen in *economy*).

This is a dynamic pattern, not a static one. Seasons change throughout each year and weather changes daily. Plant life is affected by changes in available sunlight, changes in available water and by variations in temperature. These changes affect organisms that feed upon plant life and, in turn, organisms that feed upon those organisms. Individual organisms are born and die, while populations of species rise and fall in relation to each other. In the meanwhile, spontaneous mutations arise in organisms that contribute to evolution if they are successful.

Infinite changes are continually occurring and corresponding adjustments are continually being made. The diversity and dynamism that exist within the ecosystem as a Spontaneous Order makes the whole system more adaptable to these constant changes - even when those changes are catastrophic, such as the effects of a volcanic eruption.

In the human world, there are a few differences but the basic idea is the same. Our cultures do not evolve through biological mutation - though this may change as we master the science of genetics - but instead evolve through the creation and exchange of value.

These values range from spiritual and philosophical ideas, to the nice things that we do for the people that we care about, to the goods and services that we buy and sell to live.

Also, because we depend upon this exchange of value as something that ensures and enhances our survival and happiness, we base our interactions and relationships on ideas of ethical behavior that protect and support that exchange. We do not live by the 'Law of the Jungle' anymore, but instead try to insure a reasonable expectation that our fellows are not going to kill or rob us and will rather trade with us fairly. That means without coercion or restriction.

Of course, this Spontaneous Order of society does not completely exclude conflict or competition - because competition is one of the key factors in the evolution of Spontaneous Order - but we now (hopefully) compete through our creativity and ability, and reconcile our conflicts through our reason. This is human order that is rooted in the qualities that define us as human.

And while humans throughout history and up to the present day have been forced to operate under a great many arbitrary rules, there is actually a long tradition of recognizing Spontaneous Order in both law and economics.

For example, in law, there is the tradition of Common Law. Common Law is based upon the decisions of courts rather than legislative statutes or executive regulation. The functional superiority of the Common Law system comes from the way that it *evolves*.

With regard to a given legal issue or situation, legislative or executive action does not occur until a significant problem has arisen with enough severity to draw attention to itself (assuming that the problem is not invented or exaggerated in the first place). The legislative reaction then tends to be correspondingly extreme and therefore disruptive, with frequent unintended consequences.

The Common Law, in contrast, evolves through incremental steps, through decisions addressing actual cases, in a more fluid process that gradually works out all of the details as it goes. It evolves and changes both proximately and gently in direct parallel with social life.

In economics, the sum of all commercial activity is known as the General Market. Goods and services are matched up with needs and desires, and exchanges of value are made. In a free market, the flows of exchange and the systems for facilitating these exchanges evolve in much the same way as the Common Law systems described above, and through the same mechanisms of Spontaneous Order in general: variation, competition, feedback and adaptation. Adam Smith, the author of *The Wealth of Nations*, perceived this process and famously called it the "Invisible Hand".

On this human, social level, Spontaneous Order is

often referred to as the product of human action but not of human design.

As a paradigm, the infinite variety and trial-and-error evolution of Spontaneous Order stands in contrast to the obsession with control and planning underlying what Virginia Postrel calls "One Best Way" thinking in her book *The Future and Its Enemies*, which is essential reading.

Many attempts to make the world a better place have actually caused more problems and harm because of being rooted in the view that there is One Best Way for life and society to work. Many social conflicts occur because people do not agree on what the One Best Way might be, but few ever challenge the basic idea of there being One Best Way in the first place.

This attitude does not respect the Sovereignty of Individuals or their uniquely personal knowledge about their own needs, desires and life experience. Such thinking is rooted in the belief that one comprehensive blueprint for existence should serve for everyone. Taken to extremes, this would only be possible if everyone was the exact same person living the exact same life - which is the total opposite of the differentiation that we have seen as the point of existence through Ipseity, Expression and Becoming.

This is much in line with what Friedrich Hayek called the "knowledge problem" and which is often cited to explain the impossibility of centrally planning an economy, but its veracity is much more broadly applicable than that. The essence of the knowledge problem is that planners lack full knowledge of systems that are large or complex. They lack the local knowledge of conditions and forces that are either too far away from their view or down in details too intricate for them to perceive and understand. The lack of full knowledge means that their plans will never fully account for all of the conditions and forces at work in the system, and so will always be flawed to a varying extent.

Because each Individual possesses the localest of local knowledge, it makes sense to decentralize authority to Individuals as the primary units of social systems. It is a practical consideration as well as a moral one. It is the differentiation among the participants acting on their unique, local knowledge that makes a system functional, dynamic and hardy.

Promotion of our root-values of Ipseity, Expression and Becoming maximizes the primary elements of the system: the Individuals involved.

Promoting Sovereignty and Spontaneous Order means organizing social systems in favor of voluntary relationships and decentralized, bottom-up power structures that freely permit Self-determination, creation and exchange of value among those primary elements: the Individuals involved.

7

Institutions

"The maintenance of this society calls for the preservation, optimization and further establishment of dynamic INSTITUTIONS that reflect and support all of the principles or elements described in these statements."

Broadly defined, Institutions are abstract mechanisms that organize and stabilize social order through more concrete patterns of cooperative and collaborative behavior. When Nietzsche spoke of the will to power and the need for Individuals encountering other Individuals with their own wills to power to come to arrangements with each other, these Institutions are the most basic and relatively stable forms that those arrangements take on the level of a society as a whole.

The primary and most broadly applicable social Institutions are family, religion, commerce and law. To go into much depth on these topics here would greatly exceed the space available in this essay, so it will be taken as self-evident for readers that all of these primary Institutions have been severely weakened over the past century and more. To some extent, this simply reflects change and Becoming. To another extent, however, the process is exacerbated by more pernicious influences, as willl be covered below. It will simply be said here that the mission of this project is to help dispel the social miasma created by the current rejection (e.g. family and religion) or deformation (e.g. commerce and law) of Institutions by facilitating their evolutionary *transformation* while valuing their original, core purpose.

This value also extends beyond those core Institutions. In 1831, the French diplomat and historian Alexis de Tocqueville spent much of the year traveling around the United States and observing the unique qualities of the new nation. His observations were later published (in English) as *Democracy in America*. In this book, one of the things he describes that is of particular interest to us here is the American passion for forming associations and its deeper significance. He says:

"Only those associations that are formed in civil life without reference to political objects are here referred to. The political associations that exist in the United States are only a single feature in the midst of the immense assemblage of associations in that country. Americans of all ages, all conditions, and all dispositions constantly form associations. They have not only commercial and manufacturing companies, in which all take part, but

associations of a thousand other kinds, religious, moral, serious, futile, general or restricted, enormous or diminutive. The Americans make associations to give entertainments, to found seminaries, to build inns, to construct churches, to diffuse books, to send missionaries to the antipodes; in this manner they found hospitals, prisons, and schools. If it is proposed to inculcate some truth or to foster some feeling by the encouragement of a great example, they form a society. Wherever at the head of some new undertaking you see the government in France, or a man of rank in England, in the United States you will be sure to find an association..."

...and...

"Among democratic nations, on the contrary, all the citizens are independent and feeble; they can do hardly anything by themselves, and none of them can oblige his fellow men to lend him their assistance. They all, therefore, become powerless if they do not learn voluntarily to help one another. If men living in democratic countries had no right and no inclination to associate for political purposes, their independence would be in great jeopardy, but they might long preserve their wealth and their cultivation: whereas if they never acquired the habit of forming associations in ordinary life, civilization itself would be endangered. A people among whom individuals lost the power of achieving

great things single-handed, without acquiring the means of producing them by united exertions, would soon relapse into barbarism."

Compare this with Benito Mussolini's formula for collective order, "Everything within the state, nothing outside the state, nothing against the state", and some uncomfortable realizations begin to creep into our awareness. This latter is what the term *totalitarian* refers to, where every aspect of life is politicized and administrated by the state - indeed, are seen as aspects of the state, which has become synonymous with society and even existence. What Mussolini advocated becomes more familiar every day, while the society that de Tocqueville described slips into a forgotten past. This centralization, homogenization and stasis is, obviously, diametrically opposed to what we are attempting to build with this project and is precisely what we are hoping to avoid. Differentiation, remember, is the expansive manifestation of Expression and Becoming in the service of primary Ipseity.

While states certainly benefit from the undermining and consequent failure of our private and decentralized Institutions and associations - creating a citizenry of alienated, aimless, unskilled, rootless, single, virtual orphans that will be more happily dependent upon them - we must all take responsibility for both allowing it to happen and then to initiate reversal of the trend.

The 'killer apps' of this process would seem to be what Crypto Valley founder Johann Gevers calls the "Four Pillars" of a decentralized society: decentralized communications, decentralized law, decentralized production and decentralized finance.

Decentralized communication is most important for synergy of information and is currently at its historical peak (so far) with the internet and cryptography. The early days of the world wide web were exceptionally libertarian and free, but there are people trying to change this - especially within the tech industry, itself, most surprisingly - now that it is becoming more and more a part of everyday life for everyone. Preserving the free flow of communication and information is of essential importance as it is key to everything else.

Decentralized law depends upon choice of system, adjudicator and enforcer, which was much the case in the medieval Icelandic Commonwealth as described at some length in works by David Friedman. This kind of thing can also be greatly refined and enhanced today by available technology. After all, we already refer to law as "code" because it is a form of social software. A current example is Ulex, an open-source legal system created by Tom Bell of the Institute for Competitve Governance for use in special jurisdictions and start-up communities (see the essay on Enclaves three chapters from now), which is in part rooted in the Common Law that was referenced in the previous chapter. It also does not take much imagination to see that AI and blockchain will become increasingly important in law. Blockchain already allows for smart contracts, corporate filings and notarization. Primitive forms of AI can already get you out of traffic tickets, and an 'AI Judge' has recently been rolled out in China to assist in court proceedings, though use of the term seems premature in these cases.

We see much decentralization of production already. In the old days, being a titan of business meant having the biggest factories, the biggest fleets of ships, planes and trucks, the most (and biggest) stores, and so on. Today, design, production, marketing and sales, shipping and any other aspect of business can be contracted with other businesses that provide those services. Moreover, consider 'sharing economy' businesses like Uber and Airbnb. The old communists' call for workers to seize the means of production has already been largely fulfilled today, by Capitalist entrepreneurialism and market forces.

Decentralization of production is also greatly facilitated by automation in general and 3D printing, specifically. These technologies distribute The Factory to stores, homes, the field and eventually other planets. Decentralization of materials production and energy production are the areas for further growth in this process.

Decentralization of finance relies upon decentralized currencies (e.g. Bitcoin) and decentralized contracting systems and transaction platforms, allowing for instant global payments and trade. This completes the other three 'pillars' as a process of social creation, putting social power back into the hands of Individuals and generating the Spontaneous Order described in the previous chapter.

It should be kept in mind, of course, that any technologies mentioned here or in the coming, specific essay on that subject inevitably started to become obsolete and superseded by new and more advanced options as soon as this was written.

Another social Institution that is historically important to people is mutual aid, which is now an area that has been almost completely monopolized by states as described above. This does not have to be so, especially as it amounts to another form of dependency and lack of power. While the explosion of wealth likely to be unleashed by the four 'pillars' above would lessen the need for social safety nets enormously, they can be created and maintained according to the same principles. Mutual aid societies of various kinds used to be a big thing and would provide a ready and time-tested response to people's needs again, especially if they are updated to make use of current technology. We already see a disorganized grasping at this when people crowdfund for emergency relief in cases of medical or funeral expenses, destruction of homes, legal expenses or even car trouble.

A promising idea in this area is the Distributed Income Support Cooperative (DISC), an idea promoted by Max Borders, author of *The Social Singularity*. DISCs are not a contentious (and inefficient) political program, but are voluntary and self-organizing. As such, they benefit from all the virtues of decentralization and Spontaneous Order previously described. In particular, DISCs are *communities* and rest upon a foundation of mutual accountability. Dues are paid into peer pools and claims are judged by peer juries. This makes reputation a key factor and incentivizes responsibility. There can be DISCs for all manner of purposes, for providing loans or charitable grants, with varying standards and rules, and Individuals are free to join whichever of these DISCs suit them.

One more fundamentally important Institution must be mentioned: Education.

What commonly passes for 'modern' schooling is an 18th-century model that was designed for creating a uniform citizenry and work force. It is a Second Wave system created to serve Second Wave interests. Even if, for the sake of argument, we overlook the conflict between this schooling and genuine human needs and assume that it more or less met those industrial demands as they were perceived, it is now simply outdated.

Indeed, the conflict between the 'factory school' model and education that truly cultivates the mind of the student is now an enormous liability to the very work force that schooling has intended to provide, because work now and in the future will increasingly rely upon diversity of learning, independent reasoning and nurtured creativity - especially as most other kinds of work become automated. Education in the

Fourth Wave must not only be different, it must be in all ways the OPPOSITE of what we have had. It must educate in the original, etymological sense of the word: to "lead out" or "bring up" - to cultivate the Mind-Fire.

The obstacle or bottleneck in this process is the monolithic locus of space and time called SCHOOL, and much can be accomplished by breaking it up - even the idea of it - and shifting to a cultural perspective of education and learning as things that are ubiquitous and neverending. This means a culture where education and learning are radically decentralized, differentiated and infused into most activities, for all people of all ages. This ends the segregation and abstraction of education and integrates it back into real life, while also opening wide the vista of its potential forms and methods. In this way, Education as an Institution comes to best reflect and support our root-value of Becoming.

Finally, taking all of the above together, upon the foundation of these basics, we can also then return to the creation of all manner of associations of the sort that de Tocqueville describes - updated to new means and needs - for the further fleshing out of these values and others more specific to various affinity groups.

As we close on the subject of Institutions, it will be profitable to look at two rather obscure words - *Catallaxy* and *Frith* - for putting the value of Institutions into perspective.

The terms "economy" and "economics" derive from the Greek word *oikonomia*, which referred to the management or direction of a single household. The economist Friedrich Hayek, who wrote about Spontaneous Order in economics and society, felt that these terms are actually misleading when it comes to describing the larger, more complex phenomena of markets involving many participants with diverse needs and goals. Instead, Hayek proposed the use of alternative terms like "catallaxy" and "catallactics" that he derived from another Greek word, *katallasso*, meaning "to exchange". Catallaxy, in Hayek's view, is the Spontaneous Order brought about by the mutual adjustment of many individual economies in a market.

The original word *katallasso* also has some very important secondary meanings of "to make friends" and "to admit into the community". In connection with these meanings, it is worthwhile to consider the old saying that when goods do not cross borders, soldiers will. We might also expect the opposite to be true, that when goods DO cross borders, soldiers will NOT - or will at least be less likely to. Trade being so essential to survival and thriving in life, people are not happy for it to be disrupted. This is not only true on the level of nations or only in the usual terms of buying and selling. The exchanges of value between Individuals are what form the relationships between them, and these bonds are the building blocks of social order. In the fullest sense, all human interactions can be seen as a form of commerce and, collectively, a catallaxy.

The word *frith* is Old English, with variations also appearing in other Germanic languages. Its meaning combines ideas of protection, peace and calm. Our word "friend' derives from the same root. Frith describes peace and stability but also refers to the social relationships that underlie and create that peace and stability. It also specifically has ties to the forms of decentralized law practiced in old Iceland as described above.

So, what we want to keep in mind with these words is that creating catallaxy and frith is the actual purpose of our Institutions and the actual value derived from them. We value Institutions as the means rather than the end. This understanding is the key to avoiding the 'organicist' fallacy mentioned previously.

To take a couple of steps back so as to tie the last three

essays together, it is voluntarism that is the essential factor in (re)creating Institutions that reflect and support Sovereignty expressed and manifested through Spontaneous Order as the warp and weft of the social fabric. The Non-Aggression Principle as the basis of Sovereign ethics is the true 'social contract' because it is the necessary precondition of actual society - the fundamental assurance that people can more or less go about their business and interact with each other without continual fear of being attacked or robbed. This is the primary arrangement, as per Nietzsche, of Individuals with their own wills to power creating and maximizing a shared platform for further Individual Becoming through Institutions that best secure and enhance this fundamental assurance.

Going forward, we can treat this as the primary metric of true civilization.

8

Property

"PROPERTY is the reflection and extension of the Ipseity and Expression of the Individual within material substance, and the means for preserving Individual Sovereignty within a voluntary system of social order."

Ipseity is our basic sense of Self within our own psyches, Sovereignty is our Expression of Self in society, and Property - it will be shown - is our manifestation of Self in the physical world.

Translating this value into full and tangible materiality, we have two basic areas of interest: the general 'propertarian' conception of social order developed by German economist and philosopher Hans-Hermann Hoppe, and the importance of activating and leveraging so-called 'dead capital' among the poor by way of establishing their property rights as explained by Peruvian economist Hernando de Soto.

Starting much where we ended in the last chapter, Hoppe points out that the whole point of an established social order is to minimize conflict. As an economist, he focuses primarily on conflicts arising from scarcity of goods and resources and goes on to establish the fundamental Institution of private Property as the logical and moral basis of legitimate and effective social order. His full reasoning can be found in his book *The Economics and Ethics of Private Property*.

For our purposes here, though, we are primarily interested in his description of how private property is legitimately acquired and established. First, according to Hoppe, each Individual has private, exclusive ownership in his or her own physical body. This follows for us from the things that were already said about Ipseity and Sovereignty, with this most immediate form of Property being the material vehicle of those principles. Second, one acquires Property in any goods or resources obtained through the efforts of one's own physical body prior to their being obtained in such manner by any other body - original appropriation. Third, there is private Property in any secondary goods made by the efforts of your own body from material that is also your private Property. Fourth, and finally, there is private Property in goods that you have obtained in voluntary exchange with others who legitimately own those goods as described. This last form then also extends into exchange of services for goods or in their production.

Wealth is that which enhances our existence. With the few, basic exceptions of oxygen, water and other simple survival fare such as fruits, nuts or grubs, natural resources alone are not wealth. Wealth has to be created, which requires effort or labor. However, labor alone is not enough to create wealth, either. A horse can pull a cart, but the horse can not drive the cart and it certainly can not invent a cart. The ultimate resource, the one that makes all wealth possible, is the Self-determined mind and its powers of reason and creativity.

To hunt or grow food, to build shelter and to weave cloth all required these powers, both to understand how to do these things and to create the tools for accomplishing them. Without the powers of the mind - our Mind-Fire - the metals that go into everything from a knife to a car, to a skyscraper and to a spaceship would just be rocks.

The ultimate resource is the MIND that directs labor to productive ends. The ultimate resource is the ability to look at the stuff and experiences that make up the world around us and to see how they can be shaped, assembled, recombined and redirected to produce more valuable stuff and more valuable experiences. This has always been true but will become exponentially more explicit and total with the full emergence of the Fourth Wave.

To take a step back, however, we repeat that the understanding of Self-Ownership in the physical body derives from the same lines of thought concerning Ipseity and Sovereignty described earlier. Hoppe has pointed out that even in an environment of abundance, the mere existence of bodies creates scarcity in space - two physical bodies can not occupy the same space at the same time. This self-evident observation provides a powerful basis for ethics, especially when further extended to Expression and Becoming as covered previously. This is why it is often said by libertarians that all rights are property rights - or that property is the singular right, with manifold forms and applications. Hoppe has gone into great detail on how this applies to the creation and application of law, and his logical development of these principles provides adamantine philosophical underpinning for the kinds of legal options described in the previous chapter.

Moving forward, we need to understand the latent force of what Hernando de Soto refers to as "dead capital". Around the world, due to varying interplay between obstructing policies, heavy bureaucracy and outright corruption, many poor and even middle-class people do not formally, legally and clearly own their property. This lowers the value of the assets and makes it impossible to lend or borrow against it. This phenomenon is described in detail in de Soto's book *The Mystery of Capital*. In his native Peru, he found that 98% of all businesses and 88% of all rural property were held 'extralegally' in this way, with an estimated $9.3 TRILLION in dead capital being held informally at the global level. As it stood, and stands, this massive resource can not be leveraged in the way that property is in more free and developed environments.

This leads back to what was already said in the last chapter about the use of blockchain as a public registry. In a TEDx talk on his "Four Pillars", Johann Gevers used the hypothetical example of a Maasai in Africa with no access to banks or other legal and business infrastructure of the usual kind but who can now use a mobile phone to incorporate a business entity and connect with a global transaction platform. Here, we can focus in on the specific issue of dead capital highlighted by de Soto and see a way forward in animating it.

This leveraging of trillions of dollars in resurrected capital by several billion people will not only fuel a global economic boom so massive that it is difficult to imagine, but it also lays the cornerstone of the general social order described by Hoppe when guided by all of the values described in this manual - which would all then reciprocally experience the same boom.

9

Technology

"As a material extension of personal power and intention, TECHNOLOGY is crucially important as means for facilitating the Expression and Becoming of the Individual, exchanges of value among Individuals, the transformation of environments and the general enhancement of existence."

The word "technology" derives from Greek *tekhne*, which refers to art, skill, craft or a method or system of these for the purposes of making or doing. This derives from the earlier Proto-Indo-European *teks*, which means to weave or fabricate. It is, of course, related to "technique". So, while we refer primarily to physical tools and machines in this particularly essay, most of what is described in this book can be considered forms of Technology.

In his book on the esoterics of Technology, *The Forge and the Crucible*, historian and philosopher Mircea Eliade referred to pre-technological Man as being "buried in Nature" - embedded within and at the mercy of its vicissitudes. Technology has allowed humanity to become increasingly causative over our experiences and fate, to the point that we even dare to call this geological age *Anthropocene*. Over the course of history, Technology has progressively unleashed our Ipseity, Expression and Becoming, which potentially reach their full liberation in the Fourth Wave.

The "longshoreman philosopher" Eric Hoffer wrote a provocatively-titled essay "The Unnaturalness of Human Nature" that is collected in his book *The Ordeal of Change*, and which is recommended reading with regard to several issues that we discuss in this work. One point that is especially pertinent here is when Hoffer says:

"The fantastic quality of human nature is partly the product of his unfinishedness. Being without specialized organs, man is in a sense a half-animal. he has to finish himself by technology, and in so doing he is a creator - in a sense a half-god. Again, lacking organic adaptations to a particular environment, he must adapt the environment to himself, and re-create the world. The never ending task of finishing himself, of transcending the limits of his physical being, is the powerhouse of his creativeness and the source of his unnaturalness. For it is in the process of finishing himself that man sloughs off the fixity and boundless submissiveness of nature."

When Hoffer speaks of "unfinishedness", he is

generally speaking of the same condition of human nature described much earlier by Pico in his *Oratio* that was referenced in our essay on Becoming. For us, what is essentially "unnatural" in human nature is the distinction of our Ipseity, our ability to act as our own Self-metaprogrammer (as per John Lilly) and our ability to make what - to borrow another computing metaphor - is initially 'read-only' in ourselves and our environments become 'writeable' for us. What Hoffer describes is its Expression in our lives and cultures. Elsewhere in his essay, he describes the process as being generally unconscious, at least in its early stages. What the Fourth Wave means now is fully embracing this process of Becoming with full consciousness on a cultural level.

Humanity was tending fires at least as far back as the days of *Homo erectus*, and the mastery of fire provides our metaphor for the Fourth Wave - the precision-mastery of the Mind-Fire in a more full and total way. Properly applied, Technology reflects and extends our Expression and Becoming in matter, complementing and organizing the way that Property reflects and extends our Ipseity in matter. It refines and transforms our material environments in alignment with our ongoing Becoming as sapient entities.

Many of the problems that are considered political issues today can be solved directly and neutrally by technology. On the other hand, though, technology in service to political aims is probably the worst problem that we face. What was once our liberator and source of power could become our enslaver and condition of weakness. Just as we were once buried in Nature, we could become buried in Technology.

We will see a proliferation of technologies that directly augment the powers of consciousness or/and facilitate the direct interface of consciousness with external hardware. Neurofeedback and Elon Musk's proposed 'neural lace' would be initial examples of each, respectively. This is the area of potential trouble in the Fourth Wave if personal Sovereignty and integrity are not maintained (e.g. the 'Borg' scenario). If they are maintained, however, these technologies will - without hyperbole - manifest a civilization of the miraculous.

This is why Technology is the crux that defines two radically divergent and opposed futures, both of which are rooted in two processes: *convergence* and *catastrophe*.

Convergence is the overlap and growing together of technologies. Sixty years ago, telephones, televisions and computers were entirely different and unrelated devices. Now, they have converged and fit in your pocket. Moreover, this convergence does not occur only with tools but also among technological fields. Today, we are looking at not just accelerating development within fields such as nanotechnology, biotechnology, information technology and cognitive science, but also the accelerating convergence of these fields.

Where catastrophe comes in is through the accelerating rate of convergence. The word usually connotes disaster, but we mean it here in the more general and neutral sense of the word, as "catastrophe" means "overturn" - a sudden and dramatic upheaval or change. Within the world of Technology, a convergent and catastrophic Singularity (though defined in different ways by different factions) is not only predicted but expected, eliciting both anticipation and trepidation.

In a nutshell, one way or another, an alien world is coming very quickly. It is beyond anyone's ability to imagine fully and beyond most people's ability to imagine at all, and it is imminent. Technology is the driving factor that makes our current situation rather urgent and decisive.

So, let us clearly state the issue. Ray Kurzweil, who has an impressive record of correct technological predictions, expects a technological singularity around 2045. Technology, as we have pointed out, is a force multiplier. It extends power. This means that technology will more deeply entrench our cultural values as convergence occurs. Authoritarian and collectivist values opposed to those expressed in this work are already very powerful within our civilization. It stands to reason, then, that the nature of the Future depends entirely upon our cultural values at the moment of "overturn". This means that we have much less than 25 years to shift the character of our culture for the better, lest we experience a dystopian, technocratic catastrophe in the colloquial, destructive sense of the word.

As mentioned previously, Virginia Postrel has pointed out the paradox of the technocratic focus on "One Best Way" thinking and its supporting tropes of obsessive centralization, planning and management in the face of what we have discussed - and technocrats should know - about Hayek's knowledge problem and Spontaneous Order. Oddly enough, the children's film *The Lego Movie* may provide the best metaphor for this mentality and its application. In the film - though in Hollywood fashion attributed to business rather than government - the antagonist plans to use literal Krazy Glue to fix everyone and everything in place within a 'perfect', static order.

In contrast, economist Peter C. Earle, a fellow at the American Institute for Economic Research (AIER), has said: "The future is decentralized, anonymous, trustless, uncensorable, and deflationary." We certainly hope so, as these are the qualities that will not only protect us as Individuals but will also protect our evolutionary process during the transition into that imminent, alien world.

Again, it is Technology and its exponentially accelerating increase in power and totality that makes what we do now so important. Relating Technology to the other Agathon values and harmonizing it with them is what will generate Fourth Wave civilization. Rather than becoming buried in Technology as our deep ancestors were in Nature, the integrated technocultural and technosocial domain that Kevin Kelly calls the Technium should serve to not only instantiate our Ipseity, Expression and Becoming but also protect them and serve as the reciprocal matrix and platform for their future Sovereign growth and development.

9

Enclaves

"The practical combination of Individual Sovereignty and Spontaneous Order with Property and Technology results in the formation of diverse, autonomous ENCLAVES and environments that support the fulfilment of the Good of the inhabitants and provide platforms for its further growth and evolution."

With Enclaves, we have reached our most concrete value but must momentarily return again to the abstract and talk about SPACE. For energy to move or matter to condense into forms, they need space. This makes space the primal requisite for anything to happen, for things to differentiate into things and thus for the existence of any environment.

An *environment* is defined as the total of circumstances or conditions that surround one: the combination of external or extrinsic physical conditions that affect and influence the growth and development of organisms; the complex of social and cultural conditions affecting the nature of an Individual or community; or even an artistic or theatrical work that surrounds or involves the audience. This is one of the primary dimensions of existence along with the personal-psychic and social dimensions, with all three together forming the continuum of Being and Becoming.

Traditionally, an Enclave is a partitioned environment that exists entirely within the space of another, 'alien' territory. For example, today, Vatican City and the Republic of San Marino are independent Enclaves that exist within the nation of Italy. The state of Alaska is an Enclave of the United States separated from the main body by Canada. However, we are more inspired here by the history of places like Moresnet, technically not an Enclave as strictly defined, but a small area once bordered by Belgium, Prussia and the Netherlands and nominally controlled jointly by them, but that was largely left to its own devices. Finally, we want to also marry to the term the more general idea of purposed environments and the long history of intentional communities.

To continue introducing the basics, however, two essential considerations with regard to this subject are *euthenics* and *ekistics*.

Euthenics (from Greek *eutheneo*, "to cause wellness") is defined as the science of improving the internal well-being of the human by improving the external factors of their environment and living conditions. For example, improvements in housing, nutrition, sanitation and education would be considered primary, traditional euthenic factors. This is the general frame for our thinking here.

We can then use the elements of ekistics (coined by Konstantinos Apostolou Doxiadis from that now-familiar Greek word *oikos* for "home" or "habitat") to begin to understand the 'psychogeographical' environments which are engaged, dynamic overlaps of our consciousness and the spaces that we inhabit. These are Nature, Anthropos (Man), Society, Shells (built environments), and Networks (transportation, communication, utilities and so on).

All of the Agathon values influence our approach to each of these ekistic elements to some degree but are seen most directly in our approach to Anthropos, Society and Networks - our understanding of what a sapient being is, how sapient beings ought to interact with each other most appropriately and the increasingly powerful technological networks underlying those interactions (e.g. internet, mixed reality, drones and driverless vehicles, 'smart' homes and cities, and so on). Consciously holding and pursuing the Agathon values applies a euthenic force to these elements and the others, which holisically upgrades our environments as platforms for further

Becoming.

Explicitly, our approaches in this area would differ greatly from the centralized, planned, collectivist, technocratic approaches that we so often see, because we hold Sovereignty, Spontaneous Order and Institutions that refect them as values.

In his novel *The Diamond Age*, author Neal Stephenson presents a near-future world system of social Phyles and their (En)Claves. The Phyles cohere according to a particular set of sociocultural values. The Claves are "franchise-owned (or -organized) quasi-national entities" comparable to the "covenant communities" proposed by Hans-Hermann Hoppe. An easy way to understand this model would be to imagine all of the Chinatowns around the world being under the same government or legal system rather than the geography-based ones that they are now. Another term used by Stephenson and others is "distributed republic".

In such a world, like-minded people can choose to live together in communities based upon shared philosophy, religion, ideology, aesthetics or any other system of agreed-upon values. Some may choose to recreate cultures from history or even their favorite fiction, creating something like a mash-up of the theme park and the gated community. Others may create entirely new civilizations.

At present, while we enjoy many freedoms and small diversities unimaginable to our ancestors, all of the empty space on this planet is now claimed under the jurisdiction of some state, and cultures and ways of life are becoming increasingly homogenized. Writing on this situation in his essay *The Temporary Autonomous Zone*, ontological anarchist Hakim Bey laments being born too late for the 'pirate utopias' of the past and too early for the migration offworld, saying:

"Are we who live in the present doomed never to experience autonomy, never to stand for one moment on a bit of land ruled only by freedom? Are we reduced either to nostalgia for the past or nostalgia for the future? Must we wait until the entire world is freed of political control before even one of us can claim to know freedom? Logic and emotion unite to condemn such a supposition. Reason demands that one cannot struggle for what one does not know; and the heart revolts at a universe so cruel as to visit such injustices on our generation alone of humankind."

However, as cyberpunk author William Gibson put it, the future is already here - it is just not evenly distributed yet. The creation of special Enclaves facilitates the irruption of future manifestations into the present, to then be distributed in an ideal manner as will be described below.

On a larger scale in the present moment, we can look at China's somewhat ironic reliance upon special adminstrative and economic zones such as Hong Kong and Shanghai to support their entire economy and to raise the general standard of living for the world's largest population. While this reliance certainly undermines any arguments for the dysfunctional ideology of the government, the zones have not yet undermined its actual power and they can hardly be considered free Enclaves. And yet, it is certainly an interesting development. A more promising example is Cayman Enterprise City (Cayman Islands) and there are currently other, private plans to establish much more independent 'start-up societies' in places like Honduras or even literally offshore through seasteading.

Here, we would like to introduce a term from evolutionary biology, *cladogenesis*, that refers to the divergence of species from a parent species. This occurs when a small population of the parent species enters into a new environment or their environment changes dramatically and differentiating evolutionary forces are accelerated. This is in contrast to *anagenesis*, where gradual changes occur within a species causing an eventual transformation of the whole in time.

Where this concept is of interest is in the fact that a rapid evolutionary change can be connected to divergence of small groups from the main population and to changes in ecological niches or environment. Writing at the dawn of the biotechnological era, this may apply quite literally to what we are talking about, but we can also readily see how this same phenomenon plays out in the evolution of society and culture.

Model cities, smaller intentional communities, purposed environments such as innovative schools, or any centers or facilities with activities reflecting the values of this project in whole or in part provide several important and tangible benefits:

1. They provide distinct and voluntary tests of new ideas, modes of living and technologies; being laboratories where these things can be worked out and allowed to diffuse out into the wider world appropriately, rather than being imposed upon larger populations untested and with unintended consequences.

2. They address the feeling expressed by Hakim Bey above, allowing people to live with greater experience of personal meaning, engagement and pleasure in the present day according to their own needs, desires and aesthetics, while the most adventurous get to participate in those greater experiments in new frontiers of Being and Becoming now and without waiting for change to occur on a wider scale.

3. Enclaves and environments that are established in alignment with the Agathon values will provide a differentiated, 'eutopian' bulwark against the unchecked and totalistic growth of authoritarian and dystopian cultural forces.

4. The novel and differentiated Enclaves will serve as intensified environments that can stimulate accelerated evolutionary change in the inhabitants - both culturally and, in some cases, biologically.

Archimedes said that, given a place to stand and a lever long enough, he could move the world. The creation of a wide variety of Enclaves provides us with many places to stand and to move the world by leveraging conscious evolution.

10

Creating the Context

There is a wide-ranging menu of mental disciplines and psychological practices, nootropic and psychedelic drugs, machines and other technologies that all enhance and amplify the powers of the Mind-Fire. These methodologies will continue to be important, and they will continue to increase and improve. Our wider concern, however, is in the greater ecology of consciousness and creativity within the whole *context* of lived experience.

The personal transformation that results from gains in this kind of work can not be readily sustained in untransformed environments, amidst untransformed relationships and groups. Moreover, we must not discount the ways in which transformed relationships, groups and environments provide both platforms and stimulus for further Becoming. Thus the most basic way to express our overall work is in creating the context for the Fourth Wave and the total expansion of the Mind-Fire to bloom.

Context is defined as the circumstances that form the setting for an event, statement, or idea, and in terms of which it can be fully understood and assessed.

Coming from Latin, its literal meaning is "woven together".

Our relationships create the general context of our societies, and Individuals then create more specific contexts for their personal lives within that larger context. These nested contexts create the frames for how and what people perceive, think, feel and do. It is very difficult for anyone to perceive realities or possibilities, to have ideas, to feel things or to take actions 'outside the box' of these contexts, and it usually takes something quite dramatic to make them even want to try. If new and more open contexts are created, however, new perceptions, thoughts, feelings and actions will begin to emerge spontaneously in response to the context.

While the Agathon values explicated in this section of the manual can be seen to build a linear bridge from the most abstract and monadic to the most concrete and encompassing, it ought to be understood that they are not just a prioritized list but also have a more complex internal structure. They were derived by considering three categories: root-values, organizing-values and manifesting-values. The root-values are primary, essential and ideal. The organizing-values are dynamic, engaging, connective and transformative. The manifesting values provide the base, matrix or substance of the work.

These categories were then multiplied by each other to produce nine types of value in three triads, each of which was then determined specifically. So, the first triad, the root-values, are Ipseity, Expression and Becoming. The second triad of Sovereignty, Spontaneous Order and Institutions are the organizing-values. Finally, then, the manifesting-values of Property, Technology and Enclaves form the third triad.

Moreover, each triad is composed of the three types within itself - Ipseity is the root-value of root-values, Expression is the organizing-value of root-values, Becoming is the manifesting-value of root-values, and so on in each triad. Fractally, one might say, the same transformational process occurs on each level as a part of the whole process, which is why we refer to this ninefold arrangement as an "engine" of tranformation. The root-values inform and empower the organizing-values, which then animate and transform the manifesting-values and the substance of the context.

From a management perspective, this list of values

would be seen as a complex 'values statement' - albeit a somewhat anti-managerial one. However, while the 'mission statement' of this project might be to birth the Fourth Wave in its most beneficial form, or to secure and foster the Agathon defined as the enhancement of Individual existence, the promotion of these values does not merely support the mission but is the fundamental means of effecting its fulfilment. The future will be unpredictable and, admittedly, we are working to make it more so. The Agathon Engine provides stability to the work because it is adaptable to any situation and will always be the basis of the desired context.

This information puts the entire preceding section of this manual into its own context, while also setting up the context for the next section that deals in more specific cultural contexts or strategic frames that appear to be good ones for expressing the Fourth Wave concept and the Agathon Engine in more immediate, experiential ways.

SECTION TWO:

STRATEGIC FRAMES

11

The Shift

Here, we move forward from the conceptual foundation of the Fourth Wave and the Agathon values to more strategic approaches derived from what was said in the last chapter about creating contexts. Each of the next few chapters describes a particular frame that we can both adopt for ourselves and promote to others as facets of a larger zeitgeist. The first of these - and key to the others - is The Shift.

In general, The Shift can be perfectly summed up with two excellent quotes from a pair of practical philosophers:

"The problem is not the problem. The problem is your attitude about the problem." - Captain Jack Sparrow

"You never change things by fighting the existing reality. To change something, build a new model that makes the existing model obsolete." - Buckminster Fuller

Each of the frames presented in the next few chapters is a variation on this idea. In this chapter, however, we want to look at a more specific form of The Shift by putting a personal and emotional spin on what is said in these quotes. We want to define the initial form of The Shift as a turning away from a reactive mentality to a proactive one.

A very clear example of this can be had by looking at political activism, which this manual is largely an alternative (and upgrade) to. Political activists can become burnt-out very quickly if their attention is constantly fixed upon conditions that make them feel angry, fearful or powerless. To the extent that an activist can actually create some aspect of the world that they want, they will be much happier. Even small wins are energizing. More to the point, to that extent, they are also living the life that they desire.

For example, look at our key concept of decentralization from a political perspective. This would be a fight to change laws so as to revert and devolve power from the nation to the region, from the region to the city or town, and from the city or town back to the Individual. This is a difficult fight, and gains are prone to reversals. Moreover, changing the laws would necessitate the changing of minds through mere rhetoric - a more difficult fight and even more prone to reversals. On the other hand, the technologies of Johann Gevers' 'Four Pillars' described earlier bypass that whole struggle (not entirely, but you see the point) by giving Individuals the power right away.

The Shift is based primarily on the idea that attention is a form of energy and the guide of our other energies. Our aim is the enhancement of Life, so we should never inflict one moment of needless torment upon ourselves. This being so, it behooves us to make sure that the most attention possible be directed to the things and people that we LOVE and wish to empower and enrich rather than going to anger or worry about things that we dislike or to distractions that mean nothing to us. Then, our focus should be upon creating the conditions that we desire with as little regard for contrary models or forces as possible. We are to be BUILDERS.

The Shift puts us at cause rather than effect, in action rather than reaction, and changes the situation by producing results that are immediately tangible and lasting factors going forward. The Shift increases our power and effectiveness instantly and exponentially.

However, The Shift is not just a shift within ourselves but an important one that we need to make within the world - one quite in opposition to the irritable, inflamed and even hysterical temperament of the times as this is written. Likewise, the other frames or strategies described in this section of the manual call for the same type of application. They are more specific shifts that we want to make in the culture or zeitgeist more broadly. Making them within ourselves first gives us the power to do so.

12

The Source

The Shift moves us into the stream of our causal power and effectuality. This is further enhanced by intentionally rooting ourselves in The Source of that power, remaining plugged-in to it and thus preventing our awareness and intention from getting lost in details and conditions. To even better facilitate The Shift, we should always retain the transcendent viewpoint.

The primary goal of an organism is to survive. Today, we have that goal more or less handled as a species. Food is abundant, health is well-maintained and everyday life is more peaceful than ever. There are exceptions, of course, but they are actually minimal in the aggregate. For the first time in history, the majority of the world's people are 'middle-class' or higher. And, as Peter Diamandis has shown in his book *Abundance*, this is almost certainly about to get exponentially even better.

We are moving beyond survival and into something much greater. We have the tools to create a culture and civilization based explicitly on the Expression and expansion of the Mind-Fire, moving beyond mere survival and into thriving, ongoing Becoming. However, it is a terrible irony that those tools that are the offspring of the Mind-Fire may also be used to oppress it, suppress it and even eventually snuff it out - annihilating our hard-won matrix of suvival - if we do not consciously create such a culture and civilization now. Technology alone will not exalt us, it is simply an amplifier. Our ultimate concern is in what is amplified.

In practice, the strategy can be expressed rather simply. First, remember the implicit hierarchy of values within the design of the Agathon Engine. Prioritize the organizing-values over the manifesting-values, and prioritize the root-values over the organizing-values - in both the whole and within each triad. This means that all objectives and actions in pursuit of the values should be evaluated and oriented according to the hierarchy. This keeps us true to purpose and plugged-in to The Source of our power.

Above all, always remember the Mind-Fire as the ultimate value. The Mind-Fire IS the Source of and in all of this. This prioritization of values and corresponding evaluation of objectives and actions are how we manifest a Fourth Wave civilization that enshrines and enthrones the Mind-Fire, like a jewel in a setting, while also reflecting and remanifesting it. This is what is meant by The Source as a frame or context, the orientation of everything around and in alignment with the outflow and support of the Mind-Fire on both the personal and cultural levels.

Those who work within any capacity to effect this can consider themselves to be Builders. This takes passion for one's career and fulfillment through work to its ultimate form, as a calling or path of personal as well as cultural evolution. Anyone reading this manual can determine which of the Agathon values they most resonate with, as well as which of these strategies or frames they find most appealing, and from these weave a context for particular ideas and activities that they can contribute to the process in a way that most ideally fuels their (your) personal Expression and Becoming.

In action, this path has three components:

A. Being plugged-in to inner power through The Shift and prioritization of values described here. At the moment, anything surrounding strength, power, competence and Self-reliance are so unfavored and practically feared that they almost represent the 'cultural shadow' of our times. That is why working from and for The Source is so essential and necessary. The silver lining to that is that being plugged-in makes us more immediately powerful and effective as Individuals than the people misguidedly holding the status quo or promoting regression.

B. The hierarchy of values making up the Agathon Engine and their corresponding prioritization represent a more particular form of The Shift, and an essential one in its Expression of The Source. Psychology and Education were discussed previously, and The Shift and The Source represent key strategies for their reorganization.

C. There is a definite hedonic consideration of personal fulfillment in this work. That is why we began with The Shift rather than The Source - The Shift is the way. The structure of the Agathon Engine is abstract and universal. Our own work in unfolding it into manifestation is personal and concrete. As Builders, our love of what we are building and our fulfillment in our own personal Expression and Becoming in doing that building further energizes and empowers us. The chronic frustration or 'burn out' often experienced by Builders of various kinds is a sign of no longer being plugged-in and a need for reorientation back to The Source.

As with The Shift, this strategy of aligning with The Source is also a shift that we want to reproduce in the wider world. Indeed, it represents the core transformation in culture and society that we would wish to create. The Source evokes the greatest differentiation of Individual purpose while also uniting Builders in common purpose. People working in diverse roles within diverse fields of activity are provided maximum common ground and maximum collaborative spirit. Because of this, The Source lays the foundation for the zeitgeist of Fourth Wave civilization.

13

The Network

The Network is a frame or context like the other strategies given in this section of the manual, but it is also an explicit tool. As such, it has general, topical and personal levels of application.

The flow of information has been one of the major operational concerns of all movements throughout history (the other big concern being money and resources). Today, we find ourselves in a very fortunate situation. By virtue of existing information technology and telecommunications, the ideas in this manual can be made globally available in an instant.

The information revolution of the Third Wave has set forces in motion that have deep social system effects. Advances in networking technologies are changing how people spend their time and what and who they know and care about. Indeed, this has been happening for more than a quarter of a century now. This has been the birth of The Network.

Connected social networks can quickly and easily evolve into vast, crossborder networks and coalitions. The Third Wave information revolution favors the growth of such networks by making it possible for diverse, dispersed groups and Individuals to communicate, consult, coordinate and operate together across greater distances on the basis of more and better information than ever before.

The Network is a solvent. It dissolves borders and boundaries. It disrupts and erodes hierarchies and institutions. It diffuses and redistributes power. It opens closed systems. The Network is also a reorganizer and coagulant. It is within The Network that ideas and information are developed, tested, cultivated, circulated and implemented, with new structures forming around them. Both sides of this can be seen in Gevers' Four Pillars of decentralized communication, law, production and finance as previously considered.

The form of The Network is multidimensional and organic. This is also true of its content. Both are alive, fluid, changing and evolving. In a very real way, the medium is the message.

The Network is the shift that forms the actual structure of Fourth Wave society. What biologist E. O. Wilson calls the "eusociality" of the beehive and the ant colony is entirely antisocial for humans because it negates the consciousness and agency (Sovereignty) that define sapient beings, as well as the creativity and differentiation necessary for Becoming. With the advent of the spatial web and 'mixed reality', it is imperative that formerly centralized structures and Institutions (and their accompanying mindsets) be more effectively decentralized and autonomously networked for the distribution of power - especially as the previously unconnected bulk of the world's population continues to gain access to The Network over the next few years.

Within the general network, it is our will to strengthen or form relevant topical or thematic networks of groups and Individuals with the desire, will, commitment, skills and resources to facilitate the emergence of Fourth Wave civilization through global and local activity. What "relevant" means is supportive of the Agathon values, with pre-existing networks being moved toward greater clarity and empowerment through the strategies of The Shift and The Source as required.

Personal networks can and should be created within and around the topical networks. In describing the strategy of The Source, it was said that everyone can use the ideas and tools in this manual to chart a path as a Builder that best unfolds their own personal

Expression and Becoming. To begin, you tap into your passions and cultivate relevant skills while connecting with others who share your passions and are also learning and teaching the related skills. In time, you will use your skills to accomplish deeds or create things, accumulating personal substance in your area of interest and activity. From there, you can craft your connections with others into personal networks of influence and collaboration. This is how passion becomes strength and strength becomes power.

To further assist you in these efforts, more concrete information about building Mastermind groups and creating coalitions will be provided in the third section of this manual.

14

The Hack

A 'hack', as we are using the word here, is a creatively improvised solution to a problem or simply a clever short-cut to an objective or goal. It derives from the Third Wave terminology of 'hacking' into a computer system, but is then also applicable to other types of systems or situations in life.

This basic idea of hacking has blossomed into other areas and become something of a cultural phenomenon. Dave Asprey has popularized the optimization of the body and mind through "biohacking". Tim Ferriss' book *The 4-Hour Workweek* outlines a general plan for hacking first your work life and then your entire lifestyle. In *Bold*, Peter Diamandis shows how to hack civilization. His story about the XPRIZE - which initially was a sort of bluff with no money behind it, but that opened the door to private spaceflight becoming a thing - is exactly the sort of maneuver that our description of The Hack here is all about.

For us, the great importance in The Hack as a general strategy comes from our position as agents of change confronting the previously mentioned urgency of the historical crossroads at which we find ourselves. Various forces that are either inimical to the Fourth Wave emergence or simply obstrucive of it have had a lot of time to do their thing, their structures of power and influence are entrenched and they have accumulated large amounts of money and other resources. The Hack makes us faster and more flexible, allowing us to undercut all of this. We want to hack the expansion of consciousness and creativity, hack the accumulation of influence and wealth, and especially hack TIME in the cyclical process of doing so and compounding the gains.

It must be noted, though, that the term "hack" is not always accurate in letter, even if it is applicable in spirit. When Tim Ferriss won the gold medal at the Chinese Kickboxing National Championships by gaming his weigh-in and then simply pushing his opponents off the mat, he was exploiting a loophole - a technicality in the rules - and that was clearly a hack. This kind of hack is similar to a 'cheat code' in a video game, but applied to a real-life situation. However, the business methods that he advocates in *The 4-Hour Workweek* were simply new and cutting-edge practices for doing business effectively and efficiently that are now more familiar and even being superseded.

Likewise, what Dave Asprey describes as "biohacking" is simply the DIY application of the best and most up-to-date means of promoting health and functionality. What we are really talking about with The Hack is the most adept leveraging of resources and influence.

To further the general strategy of The Hack and our use of it, we can define a general taxonomy of hacks by concept or type. We can, so to speak, hack hacking. The following categories provide initial lines of thought, experiment and implementation.

THE DRAGON'S EYE

The main idea here is that the map is not the territory. The unblinking eye of the cold-blooded dragon sees through accepted models and labels, ideologies, emotional investments and 'conventional wisdom' to the actual core and key issues of the situation. It is then possible to be extremely effective by acting in relation to what IS rather than what is thought to be.

Understanding things like logical fallacies, semantics and Robert Anton Wilson's "Model Agnosticism" are good introductions to the Dragon's Eye. This is also the key to the basic hacking perspective when you learn to always look for possible exceptions, loopholes and workarounds.

In addition to exploiting such things, another way to actively express the Dragon's Eye is to then strip away the illusory and superfluous stuff that you have seen through (except, of course, where they serve you). An example of this (in conjunction with Quantification, below) would be using the Pareto Principle or 80/20 Rule to better organize your affairs.

BOOTSTRAPPING

You can use your skills and resources to seek, obtain and create new skills and resources. It used to be said that a person that advanced in life mostly by virtue of their own initiative and efforts had pulled themselves up by their own bootstraps. This concept of 'bootstrapping' can be applied to an approach that aims to create a lot out of a little. Of course, if you do have a lot of resources to start out with, then so much the better.

Wherever you start in the process, you can progress very quickly and take it in whatever direction(s) that you wish and create whatever you want in life, expanding virtually without limit. The key is to START WHERE YOU ARE, know what you have and USE it.

Go ahead and make a list of your resources. Be as complete as you can. This action, alone, can make you realize that you are already more powerful than you might have thought. It also gives you a clear inventory of what you have at your disposal for creating positive change in your own life and in the world around you. Begin to think about how you can make the most of these resources. Think about how you can use them to get more resources. Make a plan.

SYSTEMS

Goals are important. Processes are important. Systems are what make them happen.

As James Clear puts it:

"If you're an entrepreneur, your goal is to build a successful business. Your system is your processes for sales, marketing, fulfillment, operations, etc. If you're a coach, your goal is to win a championship. Your system is what your team does at practice every day. If you're a writer, your goal is to write a book. Your system is the writing schedule you follow each week."

Furthermore, both T. Harv Eker and Tim Ferriss talk about using systems to increase your freedom by establishing systems that can duplicate and replace you (your attention, effort, time, presence and so on) where appropriate. Richard Branson has claimed delegation was fundamental to his success. Ferriss talks about automation and outsourcing.

Of course, all of these concepts can also be used to hack your own systems for even greater efficiency and effectiveness once established.

APPROPRIATION

It has been said that "good artists copy, great artists steal".

Hack those stories and creations of those who have come before you - but introduce something innovative. Especially if you are creating a product, you do not want to just scratch out someone else's name and write your own. Ethics aside, you would not really be taking the project further and would thus not be taking yourself as far as you might go. There is no need for you to reinvent the wheel - unless you are, in fact, really reinventing the wheel.

But whatever you are trying to do or create, someone has probably done or created something similar. Look for role models. Find more than one and then combine and upgrade worked for them.

QUANTIFICATION

Get feedback on what you are doing, measure your results - in actual numbers whenever possible - and act on the results.

If you are looking at something like a business or a fitness program, these things are very easy to quantify. You can look at your bottom line. You can test ads for response. You can weigh yourself, check your blood pressure or look at the results of a blood test.

However, even purely subjective things like mood can be somewhat quantified. We can say, for example, that Exhilaration > Cheerfulness > Neutrality > Anger > Despair. We can then define those states for ourselves to recognize when we are in them, then try ways to alter our mood and then measure again to look for change.

Methods for quantifying both objective and subjective conditions on these and larger scales are essential for the work that we want to do.

MAGIC BULLET

The skilled Dragon's Eye can often find one action that produces many results, perhaps even cascading results. A Magic Bullet hack, then, is one that takes advantage of this and produces multiple results or effects from one action or practice - like the saying "two birds, one stone" but taken as far as possible. A variant, Silver Bullet, could describe a simple hack that resolves a very large problem.

It is imperative that we learn, create, collect and apply the hacks that flesh out these categories, and that we do so as quickly as possible. The goal of establishing power bases and effecting great change within only a decade makes this one of our most immediate projects.

15

The Upgrade

The Upgrade is a frame for the ideal of Progress that corrects the flaws of utopianism. It is decentralized and libertarian where utopianism so often becomes centralized and authoritarian, and it is concrete and precise where utopianism is so often abstract and vague.

On that abstract level where the ideal of Progress is usually discussed, we would see it as an outgrowth of the value of Becoming and differentiation. This is fundamentally different from forms of utopianism that envision any uniform and static end-state. Those are characteristic, yet again, of "One Best Way" thinking and tend to produce a motive rooted in a singular notion of perfectibility that stands in stark contrast to our motive rooted in the infinite expansion and differentiation of Being. The Upgrade holds the 'perfect' as the enemy of the Good, and aims for 'eutopia' rather than utopia.

So, where utopianism will usually seek to produce its results in a top-down fashion derived from an abstract and vague (and usually untested) notion of the perfect, The Upgrade is a bottom-up transformation evolving spontaneously from a great number of small and tangible improvements to proximate conditions.

Buckminster Fuller sagely advised, "If you want to teach people a new way of thinking, don't bother trying to teach them. Instead, give them a tool, the use of which will lead to new ways of thinking."

Which we might view as changing the context, especially when considering the introduction of a great number of such tools.

This means many Builders, on their own initiative, working singly or in cooperation, to provide ongoing, results-oriented upgrades to Institutions and Technology, systems and environments. In distinction to the mindset of planners and technocrats, we acknowledge that these improvements can not be entirely foreseen, nor can all of their outcomes, and certainly not their cumulative result. So long as we operate from the motive to preserve and expand the Agathon vaules, however, we optimistically embrace that uncertainty.

If you have not noticed yet, this description of The Upgrade as opposed to utopianism as an attitude toward the cultural ideal of Progress echoes what was said earlier about the benefits of common law in comparison with statutory law. It is worth revisiting the essay on Spontaneous Order as a whole in connection with The Upgrade, which represents its practical application by the Builders.

When utopianism has been criticized rather than embraced, it is depicted as naive and childish at best and as dangerous at worst. In contrast, the practical "don't tell, show'" nature of The Upgrade positions it as an approach of personal and cultural maturity. To borrow a political term - and to again contrast our distinction from common politics - BUILDING or creating can be seen as the 'direct action' of the Fourth Wave as a cultural force. Our only cause to argue, debate, campaign or lobby would be for the freedom of the Builders to build.

The Upgrade makes use of all of the previous strategies or frames, but especially The Shift and the The Hack. It also immediately precipitates the next frame, The Bloom, as its precondition and catalyst.

16

The Bloom

The Bloom and The Upgrade are inseparable and yet distinct, forming a spiralling double-helix of cultural progression. The Bloom is the combined and synergistic result of The Upgrade, but it also opens the way for a broader and continuing Upgrade - and thus a broader and continuing Bloom. The mood of The Upgrade is focused and practical, while the mood of The Bloom is of a general openness to...well, openness.

This openness is of two types. The first, which largely speaks for itself, is the practical understanding that we must adopt a 'big tent' approach as Builders because that is exactly what Fourth Wave civilization is - a very big tent. That said, we can exercise some discernment. We do this by supporting whomever and whatever supports the Agathon values to *precisely the extent* that they support them - no more, no less. This is the best possible formula for cooperation and coalition without compromise.

The other form of openness, which is what will be mostly covered here, is open-endedness. The Bloom grows and changes with enormous experimentality and virality. Its form is something we can only forecast in the very near term, and perhaps not all that well. Its final form can not be described at all because it has no final form. And its blooming accelerates at an accelerating rate. The necessary psychological shift is in not only expecting this 'chaostrophy' but embracing it.

The old-order powers-that-be hate and fear this. At one point in his rule, trope-namer Mao Zedong said to let "a hundred flowers bloom and a hundred schools of thought contend" so as "to promote the flourishing of the arts and the progress of science" - which was, of course, a lie and a trap for ideological heretics to expose themselves. Uniformity, standardization, homogenization - commonality - are the stuff and substance of the communal ethos. Today, in the West, we now hear so much about Diversity, but it is a 'diversity' of only superficialities where everyone is also expected to hold identical ideals, beliefs and values - an internal homogeny.

Many ordinary people have the same fear, if for different reasons. Evolutionary history imparts an understandable animal wariness of the unknown. It is also the fear in that moment of exploration when a boat first lost sight of land. Culturally, the idea of great change can be alarming and the idea of *endless* and *unplanned* change induces an outright vertigo. These fears among the authorities and populace complement and nourish each other. Ironically, plans for utopia of the type criticized under The Upgrade are generally born of these fears while at the same time being subverted by them.

Together, they can be summed up in what is known as the 'precautionary principle', which holds that the introduction of a new product or process whose ultimate effects are disputed or unknown should be resisted. In contrast, philosopher Max More coined the 'proactionary principle', which defends the freedom to innovate as highly valuable and even critical to humanity.

This is much more in alignment with The Bloom. The fears that surround manifestations of The Bloom come from a lack of confidence in Spontaneous Order, usually because of a lack of understanding about it. Most people have never heard of it. This being so, any notion of solutions and order appearing 'magically' within society will sound crazy to many people. So, The Bloom calls for education around Spontaneous Order so that more people will understand it, have confidence in it and embrace it as a value.

To borrow a line from Antoine de Saint Exupéry: our task is not to foresee the future, but to enable it. The Mind-Fire that defines our species allows us to move beyond the animal fears of the unknown, to embrace the unknowns of the Mind-Fire's continual Becoming on both personal and cultural scales, and to recognize radical decentralization and differentiation as inevitable and desirable conditions.

Indeed, rather than being something to fear, The Bloom - when tightly aligned with the Agathon values - is our surest protection against the existential threat of supertechnologies monopolized by a centralization of power. Moreover, as The Bloom manifests and expresses itself through Spontaneous Order and Enclaves, people will have much greater choice in the lifestyles and cultural environments that they prefer as Individuals. Alignment with the Agathon values as a whole allows us to create what stability that we may need at any time without stasis.

Finally, we should meanwhile never miss an opportunity to point to anything (everything) that resonates with the Agathon values and Fourth Wave civilization and announce its emergence as evidence of Fourth Wave civilization emerging. We should compare and contrast it with outmoded examples and, in keeping with The Shift, highlight its advantages. One of the surest ways to create a particular trend in culture - and this applies to all of these frames or strategies - is to showcase it as already being one.

17

The Cosmos

Just as the Agathon values all culminate in the establishment of Enclaves, all of the frames or strategies of this section - from The Shift onward - culminate in The Cosmos. Our principles, values and models must all become tangible within our lived experience and lived environments. We shape our environments and then, in turn, are shaped by them in an ongoing, reciprocal process.

Where The Cosmos builds upon (while including) the environmental elements already covered with regard to Enclaves is in the shift from a small, closed environment and growth into a much larger (Literally astronomical!) and expansive environment through space exploration and migration. This expansion into actual outer space expands our Being into a larger conceptual environment, as well.

As this is written, the human species has taken tiny steps out into the universe beyond its home planet. The first ships have taken humans to the immediate, outer spaces beyond the atmosphere and to the Earth's own moon. Machines have been sent to Mars and beyond to act as eyes and ears. However slightly, the door has been opened.

Somewhat before the turn of the previous century, a philosophical and cultural movement known as Cosmism had developed in Russia that was concerned with the nature and evolution of the Cosmos and the human relation to it. More than a hundred years ago, Cosmism was addressing ideas such as space travel, radical life extension and even the resurrection of the dead, that are only now anything close to realistic possibilities for us today.

Together with the movement of Futurism that developed slightly later in Italy, with its calls for power, speed, electrification and everything new and dynamic, Cosmism provided a new cultural myth for an increasingly secular and scientific Second Wave society. Russian Cosmism was itself, however, a deeply spiritual movement - and, in its way, our Fourth Wave reimagining of it clearly is, too. With the Mind-Fire as the jewel in the setting of Fourth Wave civilization, and the Agathon values of Ipseity, Expression and Becoming defining the nature of that civilization and of our relation to the Cosmos, it is easy to see that this will evoke a new spiritual sense in people. The effect that will have upon formal religions both old and new can be expected to take multiple forms through The Bloom.

We are talking about an evolutionary frontier of the greatest significance. The movement of animal life from the oceans to land ranks a distant second in comparison. Whenever the human species has faced a frontier, it has been stimulated. There is a great surge of willpower and creative energies within the pioneers. There is renewal and transformation of both spirit and culture. The frontier represented by space migration can be expected to produce the same effect with exponentially greater intensity.

We know, intellectually, that we live on a planet that hangs in space like all of the other planets and stars that we can see in the night sky. However, our deep perception is still one of being bound to a flat, earthly plane, far removed from those astral realms above that we can only look at and dream about. Deep inside, we yearn for more. For millennia, our hunger for freedom and Becoming has produced dreams and myths of flight. The full realization of those dreams in the literal, physical sense of space migration will begin to alter our perspective in a radical way.

The feeling of being tied to a single, firm and daylit foundation will give way to a more open and somewhat oceanic feeling. The night sky and the stars will no longer be something that we just look up at, they will surround us. We will then be more vividly aware that this is our greater environment. With no north, south, east, west or even up or down, every direction will be Forward and open for flight and exploration.

Just as the cultural myth of Cosmism was finally starting to take literal flight in the form of rockets, a counter-myth began to emerge. This counter-myth, we can call Gaianism, and we can say "counter-" because that is how it has been used. One rarely hears an average 'Green' praising the clean energy of advanced nuclear power in addressing their concerns about carbon emissions, for example. Instead, fingers are pointed at wealthy and successful nations that do little polluting, the hopes for development in extremely poor nations are patronizingly disregarded, the proffered solutions to exaggerated problems always involve greater centralization and concentration of political power, and it is all generally rooted in a nostalgist and sentimentalist 'idealism' that celebrates keeping humanity small, earthbound and properly humble.

And the Gaian myth has been pushed by the powers-that-be while the Cosmic myth has been left to languish, only recently given new life by private interests. However, we must note that both Russian Cosmism and Italian Futurism also became entangled with authoritarian ideology in their day, and we can not assume that this could never happen again if the powers-that-be found revived use for the Cosmic myth as they currently do the Gaian one. It very easily could for reasons to do with military advantages and exploitation of extraterrestrial mineral resources.

But really, any conflict between these two cultural myths is a false and artificially created one. The Cosmos not only reconciles true and sincere Gaian interests with Cosmic ones but shows they are the same. When put this way, that the curation of ecologies on Earth and the terraforming of Mars are the same endeavor, it becomes obvious. We will rely heavily on The Upgrade in these endeavors, both in themselves and in demonstrating The Cosmos to the masses. On the Gaian side, our efforts should follow what is known as the 'bright green' track, favoring advancements in technology and improvements in efficiency and design - all in alignment with the Agathon values, of course.

It is worth briefly noting the work of Andrew J. Galambos, an astrophysicist who became frustrated with the slow progress of space travel and at the same time increasingly disturbed that his work was moving more and more in the direction of military applications - i.e. intercontinental ballistic missile trajectories. Leaving this work and seeking to determine the sort of cultural factors that would better facilitate a free and peaceful society more ready for a true Space Age, he developed what he called Volitional Science as an Individualistic and eudaemonic revamping of the common social sciences. Though he worked the problem from the other way around, Galambos thus came to an understanding of what would be necessary for establishing a space-faring civilization that is roughly the same in spirit as the program outlined in this manual.

Of course, there are a number of very ordinary, practical reasons for making space migration a primary cultural endeavor. The most fundamental is that it is a survival imperative. Catastrophic events such as the collision of an asteroid or large meteoroid with the planet or the spread of a global plague could result in the destruction of civilization and even the extinction of the species. Colonies in space, on our moon, on Mars and beyond would insure that we continue.

Extraterrestrial colonies would also provide access to new sources of energy and raw materials. For that matter, the process of space exploration has already produced new materials, technologies and industries. While this process has barely begun, our general knowledge in all fields of science, medicine and engineering has also increased due to our efforts in space and will increase further.

Meanwhile, on Earth, Kevin Kelly's Technium - including all of our cultural hardware and software - will increasingly merge and fuse with the material environment and become more thoroughly integrated through the development and convergence of 'smart' buildings, driverless vehicles, the 'internet of things', 'mixed reality' and artificial intelligence. Fourth Wave civilization will be marked by a kind of ubiquitous techno-animism.

Some have proposed that the current geological age be referred to as the *Anthropocene* due to the dominant human influence on the physical environment of the planet. However, to return to the Cosmists for a moment, the geochemist and mineralogist Vladimir Vernadsky had spoken earlier of a related idea that may provide a better term. First, there is the *Geosphere*, the basic and inanimate matter of the planet. Next came the *Biosphere*, with the coming into being of Life, its evolution and its changes to the geochemical makeup of the planet. Vernadsky proposed the *Noosphere* - from Greek *noos* for "mind" or "reason" - as the third stage of Earth's implicit evolution or Becoming.

Just as the Biosphere transformed the nature of the Geosphere, Vernadsky predicted that human cognition would in turn transform them both. He was perhaps prescient to focus upon sapience as the transforming element rather than "Man", as the emergence of AI and posthuman-beings would make *Noocene* a more appropriate term for the first three Waves and their culmination in the Fourth - the sphere and epoch of the Mind-Fire.

The word "cosmos" means "ornament" (hence, "cosmetic") and the The Cosmos refers to both the expansion of the Noosphere into cosmic space and the ongoing evolution of the Noosphere through the feedback from that expansion - an ongoing Becoming through the interplay of the Mind-Fire and the Infinite.

SECTION THREE:

SCALABLE TOOLS

18

The Mastermind Platform

Obtaining external power as an end in itself is generally quite straightforward. We all more or less know where power is and what one does to acquire it. The system or game is solidly established. However, cultivating worldly power as an extension of one's own personal, authentic, Sovereign power and cultivating power for change or innovation is much less understood and usually more challenging as a result.

There is, though, a basic underlying trajectory that can be used as a pathway to such power. It first requires Self-knowledge, knowing the code or pattern of your own desires and needs in the areas of Expression, Becoming and Sovereignty. With this Self-knowledge, you can identify your own key passions. Passion is both your rough map and your fuel on the journey.

Next, you want to build upon your passion in two ways. On the one hand, you want to learn and hone skills relevant to your key passions. On the other, you want to interact with others who share your key passions, both to deepen each other's passion and assist each other in the mastery of the skills. Eventually, you will build enough strength to use your knowledge and skills to create substance through achievements and to turn your connections and relationships into influence. When you have substance and influence, you can organize and leverage them as power.

One way to accelerate, intensify and sustain this process is by joining or forming what is known as a Mastermind group. The idea of the Mastermind alliance was popularized by Napoleon Hill in his classic book *Think and Grow Rich*, but examples of such groups can be found throughout history.

A Mastermind group can be generally defined as an alliance of two or more Individuals working together toward a common goal. Each Individual brings his or her own ideas, perspective, experience, knowledge and skills to the group. As these diverse elements interact dynamically and synergistically within the group, they play off of each other and new ideas and perspectives emerge.

The Mastermind alliance is a defined circle of shared knowledge and power. On a television series based on his works, Hill said:

"Now here are some interesting facts about the Mastermind which give you an idea of how important it is and how necessary that you embrace this principle and make use of it in attaining success in your chosen occupation. First of all, it is the principle through which you may borrow and use the education, the experience, the influence, and perhaps the capital of other people in carrying out your own plans in life. It is the principle through which you can accomplish in one year more than you could accomplish without it in a lifetime

if you depended entirely on your own efforts for success."

Mastermind groups can be organized around any shared goal or objective in life, personal or professional. You can participate in as many as you wish. Of course, the main idea here is that it would probably be very profitable to participate in Mastermind groups that touch upon enacting aspects of this manual, either directly or indirectly. The various concerns and issues in life and in the world result from a lack of consciousness, creativity, ability and freedom. Unleashing those forces in yourself and in others will initiate the process of resolution and transformation. It is both a Fourth Wave imperative and a personal one.

More explanatory and actionable information about Mastermind groups can be found in Napoleon Hills' works, other books on the subject and widely on the internet, so there is no need to go into much more depth here other than to present the idea and position it as an extremely useful platform for getting started.

Such groups are a powerful resource at every level or scale - there are business Masterminds that already-successful Individuals pay large sums of money to be members of - but they can be of incalculable value at the start. This is when you are first learning to stand and walk, to first determine your course and realize your strengths. Everyone and anyone can profitably use the Mastermind model to begin cultivating power within themselves and within the world.

19

Remedial Memeology

Everyone on Earth who uses Facebook or other forms of social media knows about memes to some extent. In those places, these are signifiers that combine images and (usually) text into a sort of DIY cartoon. These images and words or phrases are recognized by and have meaning for the audience and can be mixed and matched with each other and with new material in new ways. These cartoons as a whole are popularly called "memes" but both the images and words that are known and repeated are actually memes in themselves. Names, terms or phrases presented as #hashtags are also memes.

The "memeology" of social media is a brilliant and fantastic thing. It allows everyone to showcase their humor and insights to the world, where only a handful of professional cartoonists working for magazines and newspapers had that chance before. This has opened up a much more diverse world of humor and insight, obviously, and has notably been a tool for expressing viewpoints outside of the mainstream or contrary to convention. Contemporary references to the 'Meme Wars' and comparisons of memes with narcotics or other forms of black market contraband are only half-facetious, as whole books have been written on the role of a cartoon frog in the United States' 2016 election and certain memes can cause one to be suspended from social media accounts and even financial services in the present social climate.

All of this, however, is simply an aspect of something much larger and more complex. The word "meme" is shortened from *mimeme*, in turn deriving from ancient Greek *mimema* or "imitated thing" (hence, "mimic"). It was coined by evolutionary biologist Richard Dawkins in comparison with genes, and its pronunciation rhymes with "gene". Where a gene is a unit of biological heredity, a meme is a unit of cultural heredity. Despite the title of this chapter, the proper name for the science of memes is "memetics", comparable to "genetics".

Buttons and zippers in clothes, catchy songs, the side of the road that you drive on, sending greeting cards and brushing your teeth are all memes. Religious beliefs and political ideologies are also made up of memes and are actually *memeplexes*, sets of memes that interact to support and reinforce each other. A memeplex (meme-complex) is comparable to a genotype, the whole genetic constitution of an organism. The Technium, being the whole of our cultural software and hardware, is entirely made up of memes and memeplexes.

This is where the reification fallacy of social organicism described in the chapter on Spontaneous Order creeps in when our capacity for intelligent DESIGN rooted in the Mind-Fire and facilitated by all nine Agathon values is not taken into account. More on that in a bit.

The anatomy and behavior of a meme is like that of a virus. Its *memotype* is its actual information content - its DNA, if you will. As said, mutually supportive memes (co-memes) form into memeplexes that are comparable to the greater genotype of an organism. Co-memes that assist purely informational memes are those that act as 'bait' and 'hooks'. In advertising, it is said that people only buy two things: good feelings and solutions to problems. Co-memes that promise rewards and/or warn of threats provide the infection strategy for the memeplex and contribute to its replication strategy in spreading from host to host.

The *sociotype* of a meme or memeplex is the actual social expression of the memotype and is comparable to the phenotype of an organism. To clarify this, your

DNA is your genotype and your actual body is your phenotype. Likewise, the Bible is a memotype and a church is its sociotype. A constitution is a memotype and government processes and buildings are its sociotype. These are two common examples, and somewhat oversimplified as there are also intermediate memeplexes at work in both cases, but they illustrate the idea. Among the Agathon values - which are all memeplexes - Institutions are especially illustrative of memetic sociotypes, as one can simply observe for oneself.

Memes have a four-phase life-cycle: assimilation, retention, expression and transmission. The meme must succesfully infect its host and be held onto. It must be expressed through behavior, or it is simply an unrealized idea. Finally, to be considered a unit of culture, it must be passed on to others and repeat this cycle through them. All methods and media of communication serve as transmission vectors for different kinds of memes. What medium is best for what message, though, is perhaps more a question of art than of science.

The transmission and replication of a meme can be simply thought of as its 'catchiness', while its retention can be thought of as its 'stickiness'. Both of these will largely depend upon the efficacy or usefulness of the meme - its Darwinian fitness - but both aspects can also be augmented through other tools and tricks of communication.

Outside of totalitarian spaces (or advertising), this all goes on without a lot of thought or planning, and - in keeping with our value of Spontaneous Order - we certainly would not want to rigidly direct or control it. However, we do want to be more conscious and intentional about the memes that we host and transmit to others going forward. We want to identify and disinfect harmful or obstructive memes. More so, within the frame of The Shift, we want to cultivate beneficial and empowering memes.

To begin, just gaining an understanding of memetics - even one as introductory as this - will help to provide some innoculation by revealing what is going on. We may consider this understanding as being vaccinated with the "meme" meme. Most people do not realize that their personal and cultural beliefs (memotypes) and social Institutions (sociotypes) are memeplexes or what memeplexes even are. They simply view these things semiconsciously as being The-Way-It-Is. In contrast, understanding memes and memetics is something like the climactic scene in the film *The*

Matrix when the protagonist Neo begins to directly see the programming code underlying the Matrix reality.

Next, a sense of life purpose can be an important factor. Individuals with a sense of purpose will likely be resistant to memes that contradict that purpose or that simply do not serve it. The memes that such people do retain, enact and transmit are likely to be at least somewhat more - though not necessarily completely - consistent and organized than those of people who lack such purpose.

These two factors complement each other. Understanding everything as memes but without a clear sense of purpose can cause confusion and a lack of meaning and engagement in life. Purpose-driven memes that are not understood as memes can be toxic, as in authoritarian religious and political beliefs. However, when these two factors are conjoined, we enter into the possibility for conscious and intelligent DESIGN and we see our minds, our lives and our world as things to be created as we will through our memes. Realizing this state on any kind of social scale goes back to the Upgrade of psychology and education that was already called for, rooted in our values of Ipseity, Expression and Becoming.

While the meme might feel like the very essence of our modern Third and emergent Fourth Wave ways of thinking, a very similar concept can be found at the dawn of recorded history. This is the *me* of the ancient Sumerians, a term that simply means "to be" but that refers to a collection of concepts, roles, practices and technologies foundational to civilization.

This manual can be thought of as a tablet of *mes* for a new epoch. The relationship is immediately clear in connection with our values of Expression, Institutions and Technology. Art, Music and Scribeship were expressive *mes* of ancient Sumer, as were the institutional ones of Kingship, Priesthood and Law. These are also memes. Technologies can be thought of as 'hard' memes in relation to Buckminster Fuller's assertion that a tool will do more to change people's worldview and thinking than a mere idea. First Wave *mes* of the Sumerians included Shepherding, Metalsmithing, Leatherworking and Basket-Weaving. While the lists of *mes* are damaged and incomplete, they must have also included Cloth-Weaving, Agriculture and Mathematics. So, in the Second and Third Waves, the Steam Engine, Electrification and Computation could surely be viewed in the same way.

For us, the "Mind-Fire" is the essential meme, allowing

us to think and communicate about awareness, consciousness, sapience, reason and creativity through an engaging conceptual image that stimulates the Mind-Fire, itself, as we do so. Next, "Fourth Wave" is also a fundamental meme and memeplex that sums up all of the ideas pertinent to a civilization that consciously serves and is served by the Mind-Fire.

Then, the Agathon values and the frames or contexts described in the previous sections of this manual are those pertinent ideas and are also supporting memes. They, in turn, will have further supporting memes of their own to be determined. All of this forms an internally coherent, self-supporting memeplex that may be advanced through the tangible actions and demonstrations of The Shift, The Upgrade and The Bloom, as well as through all of the established and forthcoming tools of communication and cultural influence at our disposal.

20

Nonprofit Organizations

In the chapter on using Mastermind Alliances as a platform for building skills and making connections, it was said that the skills could next be turned into accomplishments and the connections turned into influence. This is the method for cultivating external power or leverage. While most Individuals can use this method for expressing their own genius and contributing specifically to Fourth Wave civilization through their commercial work, more general, nonprofit organizations dedicated to the actuality of Fourth Wave civilization, itself, also play a crucially necessary role in the process of its unfoldment.

Any cause or movement determines and defines a vision, mission, ideals or values and a context in the general, while providing particular niches for the personal talents and skills of allied Individuals to be expressed within that greater whole. Within this kind of broad and general context, the creation of a nonprofit organization is meant to do the same thing in a more formally organized and specific way. The organization maximizes diverse passions and talents by integrating them cooperatively around a meaningful intention.

Here is how a nonprofit organization can be brought into being:

1. The first step, if you feel called to this sort of action, is to determine exactly what you feel called to do. Corporations have formal vision, values and mission statements that make it clear why they exist, what they want, and what they plan to do about it. To begin, though, you simply want to tune in to your own general trope or direction of travel.

By contemplating the Agathon values in themselves and the relationships between the root-, organizing- and manifesting-values, you will be able to sense what resonates most with your own passions and strengths. So inspired, you can then personalize that urge or motivation according to your own interests, and this then forms a pathway of your own Expression and Becoming.

For further clarity, look for pre-existing organizations that are doing the kinds of things that you want to do. As you study them, tune in to how you feel about them and their activities, and how closely they match your own desire and intentions. If you find one that is a good match, you may be satisfied by working with them. If you do so but then become dissatisfied later, you will still have gained further clarity and important experience toward the creation of your own organization.

2. Vision and values are important, but it is your mission that defines what you intend to DO. Once you can articulate a clear mission statement, you have a reason for your organization to exist and can incorporate. This step of actual incorporation is both much easier and less costly than people might expect.

First, you need other people, because a corporation needs a board of directors. This means at least a President, Vice-President and Treasurer. You have your mission statement and will need a name for the corporation. Your board holds a meeting to agree on these things along with by-laws and any other pertinent matters. When you file your Articles of Incorporation and pay the filing fee, the corporation exists.

Even though you have filed as a nonprofit organization, you will have to separately apply for state and federal tax exemption. You have a couple of years to do this, and acceptance is retroactive. You will, however, have to include all the proper language in your Articles of Incorporaton and by-laws at the beginning. You will also need to obtain an Employer Identification Number (EIN) from the Internal Revenue Service and a bank account. None of this is difficult and there are also easily researched tools and services that can help you if needed.

(This description applies to incorporation within the United States, of course.)

3. Once incorporated, the real work begins in developing your mission into an actual, fundable program or project. For example, if your mission is providing resources to homeschoolers, this would mean something like a developed plan to provide specific curricula or technologies. This means working out all of the aspects, calculating costs and creating a business plan and schedule for implementation. Of course, you can certainly begin this planning before and as you incorporate.

4. The next step is initial outreach and pulling in of resources, both human and financial. You want to effectively communicate and market your plans to others and cultivate social, capital and political connections as needed. You want a simple way to communicate what you are doing, such as an 'elevator pitch' and/or a one-page summary that can be

distributed. You also want a web site or at least social media page with this information on it. This is also something that you can begin before formal incorporation as you clarify your plans and make them more concrete.

Increasingly today, many formerly 'in-house' tasks such as web design, marketing and fundraising can be easily hired out or crowdsourced. Expensive software of various types has become more easily accessible through 'Software as a Service' (SaaS) subscription plans. Similar models also will be making sophisticated data analytics and AI applications available to smaller organizations. In the old days, it was a big deal that small businesses and organizations could, in theory, have a web site just as nice as the biggest businesses and organizations. Now, crowdsourcing, technical service subscriptions and crowdfunding can further increase the power of small groups immensely - indeed, making them not so 'small' in practice.

With all of these things in place, your organization can now implement your project or program and grow.

5. Once you are up and running, integrate your feedback. Objectively note what works and what does not. Fix or eliminate what does not work. Document

your results and achievements and highlight your success stories when updating your media. Essentially, keep returning to Step 3 and keep refining and upgrading the rest of the cycle based on experience.

Of course, this is a simple and general overview, but we want you to be inspired. Again, while not necessarily easy, the process is simpler and less expensive than you might think. Everyone is familiar with very large and very wealthy nonprofit organizations. Because we understand and value Spontaneous Order, though, we realize that society is best generated from the bottom up. The best and most important work is done on the smallest and most localized - the most immediate - levels and scales.

21

Engaging Media

It is somewhat hard to believe now - though it was not so long ago - that only three television networks, a handful of major newspapers and a few big magazines defined the entire media narrative for the United States (with comparable situations in other countries) and shaped the general worldview for nearly everyone. This changed radically with the internet and world-wide web. While newspapers, magazines, radio and television still exist and are concentrated in even fewer hands than before, it is telling that they are now referred to as "legacy media" and are more and more overshadowed by new media and the technological polish given to do-it-yourself media Expression.

As Mickey Knox put it, media is like the weather but it is man-made. Meditating upon this meteorological metaphor in concert with the epidemiological one of memetics provides much insight on how to use media vectors to amplify your 'voice' and message once your memes are crafted and organized.

As with the other subjects in this section, the available

space only allows for this to be covered in an introductory way. Many books and other resources will need to be studied in order to flesh out this and those other topics. What this and the other chapters in this section aim to do is to recommend the subject, create a context, inspire and point the way to further research and implementation.

With that being understood, we can look at some of the major considerations in media engagement.

The most basic tool for engaging with 'old' or legacy media remains the writing and sending of press releases. Guides on how to do this as well as software and services are easily found online. Research and cultivate a list of the relevant media outlets and their contact information. Over time, you can refine this list and also maintain personal contacts made as you establish relationships. This can put you on their lists, as well, for contact when they feel you can comment on stories other than your own specific one. If you are a group, it is wise and helpful to have an articulate and mediagenic Individual acting as a press liason - perhaps several, tailored to different audiences. These basics will also serve you in engaging with new media.

If you or your organization become large and visible

players on the world stage, you will be engaging with the big, legacy media as a matter of course. They will often come to you. In most cases, though, we are likely to derive more momentum from new and independent media such as podcasts. There are a couple of key reasons for this. The first is targeted audiences. Your efforts will be in service to a particular niche and you will get the best responses when you line up with an audience that is already interested in what you have to communicate. While "preaching to the converted" yields little new movement, you are hopefully offering new things in the area of The Upgrade that inspire enthusiasm and action. The second benefit of such media is the way that you will likely be treated. The formats tend to be more conversational and are better for depth and nuance of Expression. This also makes it easier to form ongoing relationships as described above.

When interfacing with media - old or new, mainstream or independent - the most important thing to keep in mind is that the people showcasing your story or message are less interested in putting the spotlight on you than they are in keeping it upon themselves. They are giving you attention that is meant to reflect back on them for keeping their audience stimulated. Either present your message in a way that completely resonates with what the audience wants to hear and that stimulates good feelings, or present it mostly in that way but with the smallest amount of shock or controversy that will stimulate them further but not provoke outright hostility and ultimate rejection of the message. No matter how serious or dry the subject may be, you are still to some degree putting on a show. And if the subject is serious or dry, making it engaging and entertaining is all the more important.

You may wish to outright create your own DIY media to promote your other work, or you may want to become a media producer as your primary mission. The value of DIY media as it originated in underground press and even public access television was the opportunity to express diverse, non-mainstream viewpoints and spread information without being censored or misrepresented. This opportunity exploded with the original expansion of the internet and is even now still open to a great degree despite cultural re-homogenization efforts by the new media establishment as addressed below.

Within the realm of legacy media, books - like this one - do continue to be supremely important. The great news is that publishing books has become incredibly easy and cheap, especially when working with a print-on-demand service. Using such a service, one simply uploads two files - a PDF of the text and an image template of the cover - to a company that takes orders, prints the copies as they are ordered (no inventory cost or clutter for you), ships them and sends the money (minus costs and fees) on to you.

Thanks to smart phones, the equipment for a video to be made and uploaded by anyone is ubiquitous. More professional equipment is inexpensive and even expensive production software can be afforded on subscription (SaaS). This makes it easy for quality material for documentary or instructive films, interviews, vlogs and even news reports to be produced by smaller groups or single Individuals.

At the very least, you or your group will want to establish a sustained social media voice.

If your content is at all controversial - and nearly everything and anything seems to be in the present cultural climate - back it up, back it up, back it up and have mirror hosting in multiple, friendly locations.

If your aim is to produce something regular - even just a blog or vlog, but especially something like an alternative news service - the essential thing is to make it, indeed, regular. Commit to at least weekly, if not daily, content.

Along those lines, you can work with others in forming DIY networks. This is one example of the coalitions and joint ventures described in the next chapter. Your value in such a network - as is everyone else's - is finding your own unique niche or angles that contribute value, which can then all be circulated and amplified through the network. An added benefit is that when new ideas or messages get enough repetition on this level, they often eventually drift up to the big, legacy media level.

As touched upon a couple of times above, Expression on the internet has certainly become less open and free than it once was. This is certainly a crucial issue for not only the coming decade but needs to be handled sooner rather than later. As various platforms become both increasingly narrow and authoritarian in the viewpoints that they allow and increasingly arbitrary in their enforcement of vague standards and guidelines, we must create and secure ways for communication to flow freely and for information to be preserved.

Another benefit of DIY networks has to do with the possibilities of the NEW, new media and its increasingly immersive and convergent nature - virtual and augmented reality, the spatial web and all that. How soon will it be possible to not just 'tell' but to convey a compelling *experience*? To fully flesh out the the potential of such radical 'edutainment' calls for some teamwork.

All in all, the media game has become profoundly more complex due to both the cultural differentiation within society and the decentralization of the technology, both of which continue to accelerate in a back-and-forth with each other. Nonetheless, there are still just two basic modes of Expression. Engagement with establishment media is about communicating new ideas and information to people in ways that they can understand it. Engaging with more niche media is about communicating directly to your specific audience in a pure and concentrated form. These are different and both are needed. Indeed, this - and every topic in this section of the manual - invokes The Bloom in a big way.

22

Forming Coalitions

and Joint Ventures

A coalition is a temporary partnership of Individuals, groups, factions or organizations formed for a particular advantage. The word centers on the Latin *alo* which means "advance" and so designates co-advancement.

The precondition to forming an effective coalition is that you, yourself, have something to offer. On a personal level, this refers to the process of cultivating knowledge, skills, connections, substance and influence as mentioned in previous chapters. On a group level, your group must be able to offer comparable resources on a larger scale. It is potentially feasible for a smaller or weaker group (or Individual in a joint venture) to negotiate and benefit from a coalition with larger and more powerful groups, but you will at least need to have something unique to offer that will make it worth their while.

Next, we want to remember our formula for best engagement with groups or causes: that we support them to exactly the same extent that they support the

---

Agathon values. This is easy to do when reaching out to our immediate affinity groups, but our coalitions are more powerful when we connect with differing groups with differing bases. There is also the consideration of the effective competence and influence of potential partners. These factors can muddy the waters a bit, so consciously holding to the formula will help to protect the integrity of our vision and action. Be aware of groups and efforts that might seem unrelated to yours but that might still have overlapping values or desires, and measure them against the Agathon values.

Coalitions are most commonly understood as a phenomenon of politics. The publication *Coalitions: A Guide for Political Parties* from the National Democratic Institute (US) delineates five steps for effectively implementing political coalitions:

1. Developing a party strategy: The first step in coalition-building involves developing a party strategy that will lay the ground for successful negotiation. The more effort parties place on this step, the more likely they are to identify strategic partners, negotiate a good deal and avoid some of the common pitfalls associated with coalition-building.

2, Negotiating a coalition: Based on the strategy that each party has prepared, in Step 2 the parties come together to negotiate and hopefully reach agreement on the terms for the coalition. Depending on the context and objectives of the coalition, these negotiations may be completely secret or partially public. While some issues may be agreed on with relative ease, others may be more contentious and require different approaches to reach compromise.

3. Getting started: As negotiation begins to wrap-up, the agreement between political parties needs to be formally sealed. This includes finalizing a written agreement, securing formal approval of the deal from the relevant structures of the coalition's member parties and announcing the coalition details to the general public.

4. Working in a coalition: As the coalition partners begin working to implement their agreement, they will need to maintain good relations by continuing efforts to increase or sustain trust and communication among the member parties. Each party will also need to strike a balance between respecting its obligations to the coalition and maintaining its individual identity.

5. Drawing lessons learned: Regardless of whether it plans to move forward alone or in another coalition, it is important for each party to review and document lessons learned from each coalition-building experience. This will make it possible to get a clearer picture of the positive and negative impacts of coalition-building on the party and to identify lessons learned that can inform any future coalition-building efforts.

This document is a free download (in multiple languages) from the NDI website. It will be of great interest to our political activists but can also be easily adapted to the efforts of other types of groups.

Joint ventures are much the same thing as coalitions but more in the realm of business rather than politics, though this need not be so. They are a strategic alliance where two or more parties form a partnership to share knowledge, markets, assets and profits. At its simplest, a joint venture might simply be an agreement for mutual cross-promotion. Again, this idea can also be adapted to the efforts of other types of groups or even to ventures between Individuals.

With this being the final chapter of the manual as a whole, it is appropriate to emphasize this kind of collaborative effort as the jumping off point in translating all of these ideas and methods - the nine values of the Agathon Engine, the strategic frames or contexts of the middle section, and these last looks at forms of action - into explicit manifestation through cooperative activity. As the world moves and groans in its labor, the greatest ontological and cosmic transformation in history is calling its deliverers to give it birth.

This is not the last word, but merely the first.

Made in the USA
Middletown, DE
24 December 2020